I Need More Time—
And I Probably Always Will

BOOKS BY ASHLEIGH BRILLIANT

Books of Brilliant Thoughts®

1. I May Not Be Totally Perfect, But Parts Of Me Are Excellent© (1979)
2. I Have Abandoned My Search For Truth, And Am Now Looking For A Good Fantasy© (1980)
3. Appreciate Me Now, And Avoid The Rush© (1981)
4. I Feel Much Better, Now That I've Given Up Hope© (1984)
5. All I Want Is A Warm Bed And A Kind Word, And Unlimited Power© (1985)
6. I Try To Take One Day At A Time, But Sometimes Several Days Attack Me At Once© (1987)
7. We've Been Through So Much Together, And Most Of It Was Your Fault© (1990)
8. I Want To Reach Your Mind—Where Is It Currently Located?© (1994)
9. I'm Just Moving Clouds Today—Tomorrow I'll Try Mountains© (1998)
10. I Need More Time, And I Probably Always Will© (2019)

Other Books

The Great Car Craze: How Southern California Collided With The Automobile In The 1920's (1989)

Be A Good Neighbor, And Leave Me Alone:© Essays And Other Wry And Riotous Writings (1992)

I Need More Time – And I Probably Always Will

by

Ashleigh Brilliant

Author: Ashleigh Brilliant
117 West Valerio Street
Santa Barbara, California 93101-2927

ISBN: 978-1-7333518-1-2

BRILLIANT PHOTO CREDIT: Brian Stains

KIERAN PUBLISHING
P.O. Box 3863
Santa Barbara, CA 93130
www.Kieranpublishing.com

DEDICATION:

To the memory of my wife Dorothy (1931-2018) who was, and will always be, so much a part of all my work.

And to the memory of Howard Weeks (1924-2013) the best publisher and friend I could ever have hoped for.

Pot-Shots
BY ASHLEIGH BRILLIANT
©ASHLEIGH BRILLIANT 2003.
POT-SHOTS NO. 9481.
MY BEST SIDE
IS ON THE INSIDE.
ashleighbrilliant.com

Contents

I LIVE IN A WORLD OF MY OWN,

BUT VISITORS ARE ALWAYS WELCOME.

Ashleigh Brilliant

Introduction:

Welcome back! (Or is it *you* who should be welcoming *me* back?) This is the tenth collection of my Brilliant Thoughts (also known as Pot-Shots), in a series which began, in 1979, with a volume called *I May Not Be Totally Perfect, But Parts of Me Are Excellent*. But, ever since the ninth volume appeared in 1999, the need to complete my own version of a Decalogue, by adding one more to the series, has been pressing upon my mind.

Why the long hiatus? Mainly because Howard Weeks, the Publisher of all nine of those previous collections, under the Company name of Woodbridge Press — who was a good person in every way, and a *specially* good friend to me — and to whose memory this book is, in part, fondly dedicated — retired, and his firm went out of business.

I continued producing Pot-Shots for use in other media, particularly syndication, until they totaled 10,000 (which I felt should be enough to satisfy anyone's possible need). I then stopped publishing new ones — though nothing could stop me from continuing to write them — and I have kept the entire original range of 10,000 in print on postcards. But I never sought another book publisher, feeling that Howard Weeks, and Woodbridge, were somehow an irreplaceable part of my life. In the meantime, however, the entire concept of book production and distribution has undergone many changes — and this present work may reach you by means which hardly existed when its predecessors were first published.

As might be expected, my career over these last 20 years, as the world's only full-time professional epigrammatist, has continued to be dappled with remarkable developments, of which it is now my agreeable task to give you a small sampling.

Wise Guise

In 2009 a distinguished author named Henry Alford published a book he called *How To Live: A Search for Wisdom from Old People.*[1] I was then in my mid-seventies, and was only one of many people, some of them quite famous, whom Mr. Alford chose to interview. But, when the book came out, I found, to my astonishment, that he had made *me* the climax of his search for wisdom, and actually devoted his entire concluding section to discussing my epigrams, and his visit to my home in Santa Barbara.

Just as extraordinary, in its way, was an official proclamation issued in 2013 by the City of Santa Barbara, on my 80th birthday, and signed by the Mayor, honoring me as the "Wise Old Man of the Mountain." (I don't actually live on a mountain, but the celebration was held on one.)

City of Santa Barbara

Here's wishing you a very Happy 80th Birthday!
December 9, 1933

Ashleigh Brilliant

Wise Old Man of the Mountain

Helene Schneider
Mayor
December 9th, 2013

Of course, I appreciate any such favorable notice, but I'm very skeptical about "wisdom." After all, what is it really worth? If I'm so wise, why aren't I rich — and why do I still seem so far from my long-stated goal of the Nobel Prize for Literature? (There is unfortunately no such prize purely for Wisdom — but of course, a truly wise person wouldn't care.) However, a milestone, of sorts, was, set on September 13, 2013, when David Peacock, himself an artist and poet, helped establish a monetary value for my "wisdom," by paying me $100 — for an original illustrated epigram on a subject

1 *NewYorkTwelve: Hachette Book Group*

of his choice — the most anyone had, until then, ever forked over for any single piece of my work. The subject chosen was "Art." Mr. Peacock, who, of course, now owns the piece, has kindly permitted me to share the result with you: "The true artist waits for the right moment — But the right moment never waits for anybody."

User Friendly

Meanwhile, my work has continued to find itself being used in odd ways, and in odd places, from ice cream advertisements ("What did people do for pleasure before Ice Cream was invented?"[2]) to library cards ("The closest you will ever come in this life to an orderly universe is a good library."[3]) to San Francisco hotel rooms ("There may be no Heaven anywhere — but somewhere there is a San Francisco."[4])

---

2 *McConnell's Ice Cream, Santa Barbara, California, 2015*

3 *Stratford, Connecticut, Public Library, 2006*

4 *Savoy Hotel, Geary St., 2005*

POT-SHOTS NO. 1101

WHAT DID PEOPLE DO FOR PLEASURE

BEFORE ICE-CREAM WAS INVENTED?

Ashleigh Brilliant

POT-SHOTS NO. 3245.

Ashleigh Brilliant

THE CLOSEST YOU WILL EVER COME IN THIS LIFE TO AN ORDERLY UNIVERSE IS A GOOD LIBRARY.

In the world of Fashion and Design, among my Pot-Shots licensees, I can now list such names as Zara, (ladies' T-shirts, 2007) and Marc Jacobs (tote-bags and stationery, 2014).

Awful If Not Lawful

As is well-known, I have always been zealously protective of my copyrights and trademarks — and there have, thus far in this century, been two cases of particular note. One involved my trademark, "Brilliant Thoughts," which of course has the special virtue of incorporating my own actual name. I thought it unlikely that anyone else would dare to tread on that territory. But — wouldn't you know it — the new millennium had barely begun when somebody brought out a book called "The Most Brilliant Thoughts of All Time" — and they even had the audacity to subtitle it, "In Two Lines or Less," echoing my own tag-line of "in seventeen words or less." The publisher was no nonentity, but the eminent Harper Collins, who should have known better. (All registered trademarks can be fairly easily checked.) As usually happens, the case was eventually settled out of court for "a substantial sum."

Then came an even more sensational case, which involved that giant of the greeting card industry, the Hallmark Company. At some recent point, they had decided to stop using their old trademark slogan, "If You Care Enough to Send the Very Best," and adopted a new one: "Life Is a Special Occasion." Now it so happened that, in 1975, I had copyrighted Pot-Shot #641, which says "Life Is a Very Special Occasion." The case was complicated by the fact that for several years in the 1980's, Hallmark had been one of my official licensees, with full access to all my work. They hadn't used #641 then, but this new usage appeared years after our license contract had expired — without any consultation with me, let alone any attribution or payment. Once again, as in many of these cases, there was eventually an out-of-court settlement, with an undisclosed payment, for which I had to permit continued use of the line, with no acknowledgment of my authorship. But I know — and now you know — where they got it.

That's Me All Over

Pot-Shots have continued to appear in a variety of publications, of which one of the most remarkable is a 2004 book, *Postcards From the Boys*, (San Francisco: Chronicle Books) a collection of cards sent to Ringo Starr, the Beatles' drummer, from the other 3 members of that world-famous musical group. One, sent by John Lennon from New York, is Pot-Shot #34, which says "LET'S LOVE ONE ANOTHER, AND GET IT OVER WITH." John's comment, written on the other side, was "This is the truth as we see it."

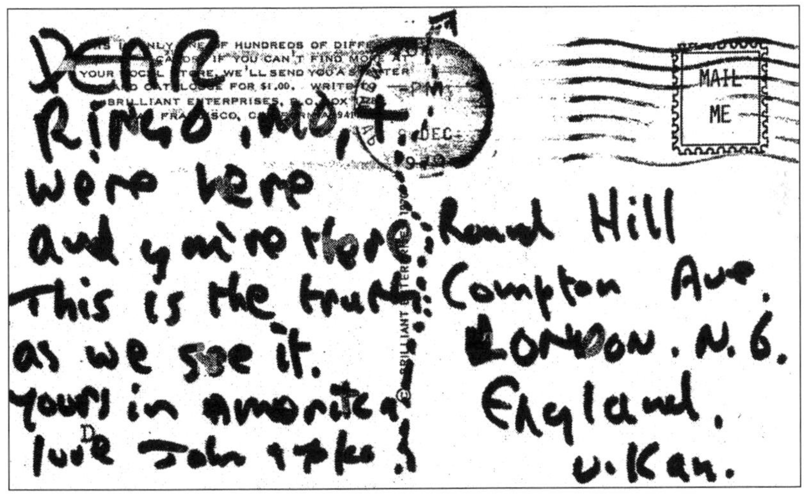

I have also appeared in an increasing number of collections of works variously characterized as "epigrams," "aphorisms," and "quotations." A notable example is James Geary's *Guide to the World's Great Aphorists,* (2007) in which I share honors with Buddha and Woody Allen.

Then there is the remarkable series of "Furry Logic" books (Berkeley, Ten Speed Press), beautifully illustrated with animal pictures, by the gifted New Zealand painter, Jane Seabrook — in which the creatures are matched with carefully-chosen Pot-Shots. For instance, a lovely "tabby cat," licking its paw, has the message, "If you take care of yourself, that will be one less person you have to worry about." (Pot-Shot #8712).

Nowadays, of course, if you're not to be found "online," you hardly exist. Besides my own website, since April 2015, a different Pot-Shot has been appearing every day of the year on GoComics.com, a site which brings together most of the best-known features in the world of comics and related material. I have never considered myself a "cartoonist," and Pot-Shots doesn't neatly fit into any conventional category — but it's good to be so widely accessible this way, even if I am competing for attention with hundreds of other "creators."

Back to School

My dream of being welcomed back with honor and acclaim by the many schools and colleges where I have studied or taught has so far been realized twice. The first occasion was in May, 2000, when — at what is now Claremont Graduate University (in my time, some 45 years earlier, it was Claremont Graduate School) I was welcomed back as that year's "Distinguished Alumnus."

Two years later, there was a much more sensational "homecoming," at Central Oregon Community College, in Bend, where I'd been a Professor nearly 40 years previously. I had had to leave in disgrace, after generating a "Free Speech" furor over certain words (particularly in Alan Ginsberg's *Howl*) presented in a poetry group I had organized. But now, in the light of my subsequent fame, all was forgiven, and documents relating to what had become known as "The Brilliant Affair" were archived among the "Special Collections" of the College library.

So, there you have some of the highlights which have illuminated the long dark interval between Volumes 9 and 10. Of course I have been careful to avoid mentioning any of the lowlights — the failures and disappointments — but I trust you will get more than a flavor of those from the dollops of alleged "wisdom" which follow.

Rule of Some

But let me just re-state, for those who need them, some of the principal self-imposed rules which I hope give my work its distinctive character:

Pot-Shots must be no longer than 17 words (but there's no minimum).

They must be easy to translate into other languages.

The words may always be appreciated on their own, without requiring any illustration.

Topical or cultural references are avoided, for maximum understanding in any place or time.

Originality is important, and so is avoiding self-repetition.

There is no restriction on subject matter, but whatever is said should be really worth saying, and said in the best possible way.

See You in My Themes

It was the title (Pot-Shot #407) which suggested the theme of TIME for this volume. But who cares? Nobody has ever commented on any of the previous themes – and the disparate Brilliant Thoughts gathered here, and so carefully organized into chapters, scarcely anticipated being reduced to any sort of order.

That business being taken care of, please consider yourself now well and truly introduced to what follows.

# # #

©BRILLIANT ENTERPRISES 1973

POT-SHOTS NO. 407

Ashleigh Brilliant

I NEED MORE TIME

AND I PROBABLY ALWAYS WILL.

1. It's About Time

In this age of nano-seconds and light-years, time is no longer what it used to be. Any attempt to answer the simple question, "When?" may involve so many complexities that you may never have time to deal with "Where?" and "How?"— to say nothing of "Why?"

But we hardly have time to think about time anyway—because, as everybody knows, the process of thinking is notoriously fast. "Quick as thought" is one of those time-honored expressions we are prone to accept without thinking, although the process of thinking things out, or thinking them through, is actually one which may often require more time than you have available.

Nevertheless, this is a book of "Brilliant Thoughts," which in fact took a lifetime to germinate, and find their way from my head into yours. And many of those thoughts, as presented in this chapter, are related to Time, and its brother, Change, in whose shadow we live constantly, without ever really understanding who they are, and what motivates them.

However different you and I may be from each other, one thing we share is that of going together through this mysterious experience called Life. Since ultimately Life is whatever we think it is, I can only hope that these thoughts of mine may have some stimulating effect on your own thinking, and that, in looking them over, you may even find yourself having a good Time.

POT-SHOTS NO. 9299.

I'M HAPPY LIVING IN THIS PLACE CALLED TODAY ~

BUT MY LEASE EXPIRES AT MIDNIGHT.

ashleighbrilliant.com

POT-SHOTS NO. 9897.

THE ONLY LIGHT WE HAVE TO READ THE FUTURE

IS THE DIM LIGHT OF THE PAST.

ashleighbrilliant.com

POT-SHOTS NO. 8167.

LIVING A SINGLE DAY IS SUCH AN OVERWHELMING EXPERIENCE ~

HOW CAN I EVER LIVE A WHOLE LIFETIME?

www.ashleighbrilliant.com

© ASHLEIGH BRILLIANT 2003.
POT-SHOTS NO. 9568.
I WANT TO MAKE SOME CHANGES
IN MY DESTINY.
ashleigh Brilliant.com

© ASHLEIGH BRILLIANT 1998. SANTA BARBARA
POT-SHOTS NO. 8165.
DIFFICULT AS IT IS,
I HAVE TO BE SOMEWHERE EVERY MINUTE OF EVERY DAY.
ashleigh Brilliant

© ASHLEIGH BRILLIANT 2003
POT-SHOTS NO. 9322.
WILL YOU STILL LOVE ME
WHEN YOU CAN'T REMEMBER
WHO I AM?
ashleigh Brilliant .com

©ASHLEIGH BRILLIANT 1999. SANTA BARBARA.
POT-SHOTS NO. 8380.
www.AshleighBrilliant.com
TODAY CAN DO SO MUCH FOR TOMORROW ~
HOW SAD THAT TOMORROW CAN DO SO LITTLE FOR TODAY.

©ASHLEIGH BRILLIANT 1999. SANTA BARBARA.
POT-SHOTS NO. 8196.
HOW CAN IT BE
TODAY
ALREADY?
www.AshleighBrilliant.com

©ASHLEIGH BRILLIANT 2005.
POT-SHOTS NO. 9797.
AshleighBrilliant.com
HOW OLD YOU FEEL MATTERS MORE THAN HOW OLD YOU ARE ~
EXCEPT IN A COURT OF LAW.

©ASHLEIGH BRILLIANT 1999, SANTA BARBARA.
POT-SHOTS NO. 8375.
THIS WORLD IS EASY TO ESCAPE FROM ~
PROVIDED YOU'RE NOT INTERESTED IN COMING BACK.
www.AshleighBrilliant.com

©ASHLEIGH BRILLIANT 1999, SANTA BARBARA.
POT-SHOTS NO. 8256.
www.AshleighBrilliant.com
THE LONGER THINGS GO ON AS THEY ARE,
THE MORE LIKELY IT IS THAT SOMETHING WILL CHANGE.

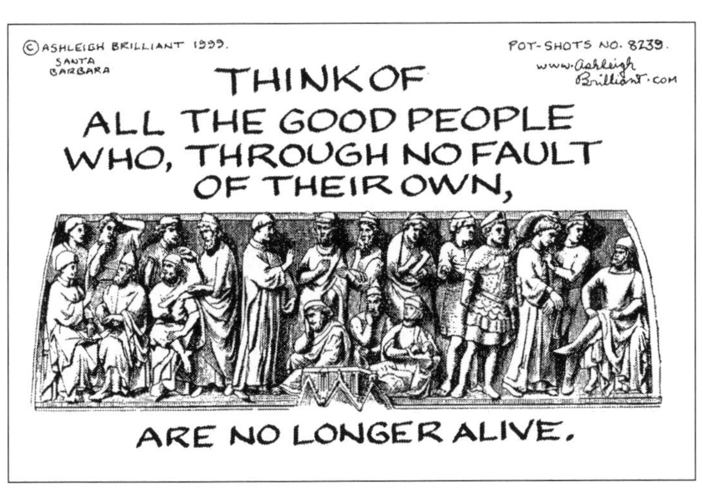
©ASHLEIGH BRILLIANT 1999. SANTA BARBARA
POT-SHOTS NO. 8239.
www.AshleighBrilliant.com
THINK OF ALL THE GOOD PEOPLE WHO, THROUGH NO FAULT OF THEIR OWN,
ARE NO LONGER ALIVE.

©ASHLEIGH BRILLIANT 2003. POT-SHOTS NO. 9248.

TWO THINGS ABOUT THE FUTURE ARE ABSOLUTELY CERTAIN:

(1) IT'S COMING

(2) IT ISN'T HERE YET.

AshleighBrilliant.com

©ASHLEIGH BRILLIANT 2005. POT-SHOTS NO. 9809.

THE PEOPLE WE WERE NEVER CHANGE~

BUT THE PEOPLE WE ARE NEVER STOP CHANGING.

AshleighBrilliant.com

©ASHLEIGH BRILLIANT 2003. POT-SHOTS NO. 9264.

WE WANT EVERYTHING SPEEDED UP,

EXCEPT SEX AND AGING.

AshleighBrilliant.com

©ASHLEIGH BRILLIANT 2003. POT-SHOTS NO. 9134.

I'LL
SEE YOU
LATER ~

BUT
I'D RATHER
SEE YOU
SOONER.

AshleighBrilliant.com

©ASHLEIGH BRILLIANT 2003. POT-SHOTS NO. 9165.

IT TAKES
SOME OF US
A LONG TIME

TO FINISH
BEING OLD.

Ashleigh
Brilliant.com

©ASHLEIGH BRILLIANT 1999. SANTA BARBARA. POT-SHOTS NO. 8313.

WHEREVER
YESTERDAY
WENT,

IT TOOK
SOME OF ME
WITH IT.

www.
Ashleigh
Brilliant
.com

©ASHLEIGH BRILLIANT 2003.
POT-SHOTS NO. 9430.
LIFE
CLINGS TO US
AS LONG
AS IT CAN ~
and then
it lets
us go
AshleighBrilliant.com

©ASHLEIGH BRILLIANT 1999 SANTA BARBARA
POT-SHOTS NO. 8395.
www.AshleighBrilliant.com
SOCIETY
IS THE PENALTY PEOPLE MUST PAY,
IF THEY CAN'T COPE WITH SOLITUDE.

2. People Time

It is now Time for us to consider Humanity, whose time-span on Earth has so far been relatively brief—and nobody knows how much farther it will extend. But we are all somehow involved in its destiny.

You can think of Humanity as a whole, or of any entity within it, as some kind of a family. This applies to an entire nation, and goes all the way down to a single individual (a "family of one.") But the units most likely to be called families are those who most feel that they belong together, and who are most "familiar" with one another. Such groupings can include people and pets — and depending on how far you want to stretch your mental muscles, they can also include friends, and even strangers. (After all, every family member was once a stranger.)

So, welcome to People-Land, otherwise known as "Society" or "Everybody." What makes it hard to think objectively about this very non-exclusive club is that the Author, your resident thinker, happens to be a card-carrying member himself. And the cards so carried — each bearing a single thought — now number precisely 10,000.

All of those 10,000 messages, including all the thoughts in this chapter, originally appeared as postcards, starting in 1967 — and to this day, they are still available (and mailable) in that form.

But people are notoriously apt to perceive time in different ways, depending on what they are currently experiencing. Good times whiz by, while bad times drag. No royal decree or Act of Congress can do anything about it. As far as this book is concerned, I can only recommend that, for maximum absorption, you take only a little at a time.

©ASHLEIGH BRILLIANT 1999 SANTA BARBARA
POT-SHOTS NO. 8455.
PEOPLE THINK THERE'S SOMETHING SPECIAL ABOUT PEOPLE ~
www.AshleighBrilliant.com
JUST AS PIGS THINK THERE'S SOMETHING SPECIAL ABOUT PIGS.

©ASHLEIGH BRILLIANT.COM
POT-SHOTS NO. 9865.
AshleighBrilliant.com
THE FAULTS OF SOME PEOPLE
ARE AMONG THEIR MOST ATTRACTIVE FEATURES.

©ASHLEIGH BRILLIANT 2005.
POT-SHOTS NO. 9717.
AshleighBrilliant.com
SEX IS EASY.
LOVE IS HARD.
MARRIAGE IS VERY HARD.
AND CHILDREN ARE IMPOSSIBLE.

©ASHLEIGH BRILLIANT 2003.
POT-SHOTS NO. 9645.
NOBODY CARES HOW YOU FEEL,
SO LONG AS YOUR PERFORMANCE DOESN'T SUFFER.
AshleighBrilliant.com

©ASHLEIGH BRILLIANT 1999. SANTA BARBARA.
POT-SHOTS NO. 8210.
IT'S UNFAIR!
BY THE TIME CHILDREN ARE READY
TO RUN THEIR OWN LIVES,
THEY'RE NO LONGER CHILDREN.
www.AshleighBrilliant.com

©ASHLEIGH BRILLIANT 2003.
POT-SHOTS NO. 9442.
WHY DO PEOPLE AVOID ME,
WHEN I KEEP TELLING EVERYONE HOW NICE I AM?
AshleighBrilliant.com

©ASHLEIGH BRILLIANT 2003

POT-SHOTS NO. 9493.

THERE'S NEVER ENOUGH TIME TO BE A CHILD,

BEFORE THEY START MAKING YOU GROW UP.

AshleighBrilliant.com

©ASHLEIGH BRILLIANT 2001

POT-SHOTS NO. 8746.

LET'S START A SECRET PROTEST MOVEMENT,

AND NOT LET ANYONE KNOW WHAT WE'RE PROTESTING!

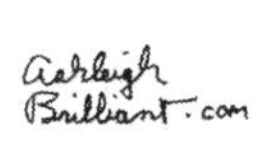

©ASHLEIGH BRILLIANT 1999.
POT-SHOTS NO. 8223.
SOME PEOPLE NEVER FEEL MORE AT HOME
www.AshleighBrilliant.com
THAN WHEN THEY'RE MOVING FROM PLACE TO PLACE.

©ASHLEIGH BRILLIANT 1999. SANTA BARBARA.
POT-SHOTS NO. 8509.
FRIENDS ARE FRIENDS BECAUSE THEY WANT TO BE ~
FAMILY'S FAMILY, WHETHER IT WANTS TO BE, OR NOT
www.AshleighBrilliant.com

©ASHLEIGH BRILLIANT 1999. SANTA BARBARA.
POT-SHOTS NO. 8293.
IN ORDER TO BE THE ONE SELECTED,
www.AshleighBrilliant.com
IT'S SOMETIMES GOOD ENOUGH TO BE EVERYBODY'S SECOND CHOICE.

©ASHLEIGH BRILLIANT 2005. POT-SHOTS NO. 9900.

YOUR PARENTS AREN'T ALWAYS RIGHT,

BUT THEY BECOME LESS WRONG AS YOU GET OLDER.

ashleighbrilliant.com

©ASHLEIGH BRILLIANT 1999. SANTA BARBARA.
POT-SHOTS NO. 8366.
THERE ARE THINGS YOU CAN HAVE AND NEVER USE ~
BUT FREEDOM IS NOT ONE OF THEM.
www.AshleighBrilliant.com

©ASHLEIGH BRILLIANT 2003.
POT-SHOTS NO. 9155.
CHILDHOOD LASTS ONLY A FEW YEARS ~
BUT THOSE YEARS MAKE ALL THE DIFFERENCE TO ALL THE REST.
AshleighBrilliant.com

©ASHLEIGH BRILLIANT 1999 SANTA BARBARA
POT-SHOTS NO. 8397.
HOW CAN I PROTECT MY CHILD
FROM THE DANGER OF BEING OVER-PROTECTED?
www.AshleighBrilliant.com

©ASHLEIGH BRILLIANT 1999. SANTA BARBARA.
POT-SHOTS NO. 8317.
THE NUMBER OF PEOPLE WHO BELIEVE IT
HAS NO BEARING ON WHETHER OR NOT IT IS TRUE.
www.AshleighBrilliant.com

©ASHLEIGH BRILLIANT 2001
POT-SHOTS NO. 9003.
IF ONLY THE WORLD'S DEMAND FOR STUPIDITY
WERE AS GREAT AS THE SUPPLY!
AshleighBrilliant.com

©ASHLEIGH BRILLIANT 1999. SANTA BARBARA.
POT-SHOTS NO. 8611.
PROMISE ME YOU WON'T DO IT AGAIN~
OR AT LEAST BE MORE CAREFUL NOT TO GET CAUGHT.
www.AshleighBrilliant.com

© ASHLEIGH BRILLIANT 2001
POT-SHOTS NO. 9006.
THE HIGHEST PRODUCT OF THE HUMAN BRAIN
WAS THE INVENTION OF GOOD MANNERS.
AshleighBrilliant.com

© ASHLEIGH BRILLIANT 1999. SANTA BARBARA.
POT-SHOTS NO. 8307.
A CHAIN'S AS STRONG AS ITS WEAKEST LINK ~
BUT A FAMILY'S AS STRONG AS ITS STRONGEST MEMBER.
www.AshleighBrilliant.com

© ASHLEIGH BRILLIANT 2003.
POT-SHOTS NO. 9546.
WHY IS NOBODY EVER KEPT AWAKE
BY A BABY LAUGHING?
AshleighBrilliant.com

©ASHLEIGH BRILLIANT 1999. SANTA BARBARA. POT-SHOTS NO. 8412.

WHY ARE
BORING PEOPLE

ALWAYS
SO WILLING
TO SHARE
SO MUCH OF
THEMSELVES?

www.AshleighBrilliant.com

©ASHLEIGH BRILLIANT 2005. POT-SHOTS NO. 9830.

AshleighBrilliant.com

BEING
HUMAN
IS MY
EXCUSE~

WHAT'S
YOURS?

©ASHLEIGH BRILLIANT 2005. POT-SHOTS NO. 9189.

ashleighBrilliant.com

ANY PLACE
WHERE MANY PEOPLE
COME
AND GO

IS PROBABLY
EXCITING,
DANGEROUS,

AND HARD
TO KEEP
CLEAN.

©ASHLEIGH BRILLIANT 2003.
POT-SHOTS NO. 9440.
I NEVER THOUGHT I'D FIND IT SO HARD
TO MAKE A GOOD IMPRESSION ON MY PARENTS.
Ashleigh Brilliant .com

©ASHLEIGH BRILLIANT 1999. SANTA BARBARA.
POT-SHOTS NO. 8403.
WE MUST NEVER LOSE SIGHT OF THE FACT THAT...
— I'M SORRY— I'VE JUST LOST SIGHT OF IT.
www.Ashleigh Brilliant.com

©ASHLEIGH BRILLIANT 1999. SANTA BARBARA.
POT-SHOTS NO. 8662.
MEN AND WOMEN CAN DECEIVE YOU~
CHILDREN CAN FORGET YOU~
THANK GOD THERE ARE DOGS.
www.Ashleigh Brilliant.com

 POT-SHOTS NO. 8303.

CONSIDERING EVERYTHING,

I CAN'T POSSIBLY CONSIDER EVERYTHING.

www.AshleighBrilliant.com

 POT-SHOTS NO. 9495.

THE ONLY KNOWN WAY OF IMPROVING THE FUTURE

IS CALLED PLANNING.

AshleighBrilliant.com

3. How Long, O Lord!

Let us now take a little Time to think about thinking. Any thinker worthy of your attention has to be ready both to gaze down into the most daunting darkness, and to look upward, and outward, daring to be dazzled by the light. In the following pages you will find thoughts too serious to be taken lightly and others (or the same ones) too light to be taken seriously. If any seem foreign to your own way of looking at things, be glad someone else has been doing the thinking which you might otherwise have had to do for yourself.

How do I think of these things? If it were a teachable process, there might be commercial possibilities in giving Thinking Lessons. But the scanty offerings of that type currently available seem mostly to harp on "Critical Thinking"— as if the role of the dedicated thinker were always to be some kind of a critic — at best, a connoisseur, at worst, a mere fault-finder. But in my own experience, the best thoughts come without rhyme or reason, and certainly without conscious intention.

If you can handle ideas about religion and reality, morality and mortality, existence and exasperation, you should be able to make it safely through this chapter. Otherwise, of course, you can always go all the way around it (if you have the time.)

©ASHLEIGH BRILLIANT 1999. SANTA BARBARA.
POT-SHOTS NO. 8456.
www.AshleighBrilliant.com
COMPLETE ETHICS COURSE:
WILL IT DO ANY HARM?
MIGHT I GET CAUGHT?
WHAT WOULD MY MOTHER SAY?

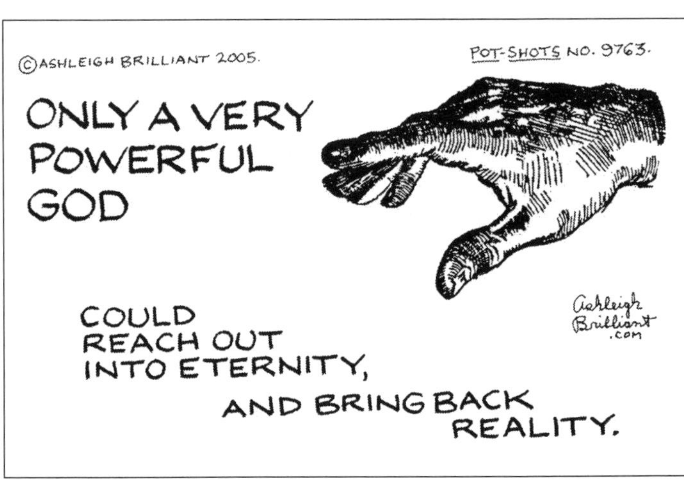
©ASHLEIGH BRILLIANT 2005.
POT-SHOTS NO. 9763.
ONLY A VERY POWERFUL GOD
AshleighBrilliant.com
COULD REACH OUT INTO ETERNITY,
AND BRING BACK REALITY.

©ASHLEIGH BRILLIANT 2001
POT-SHOTS NO. 8835.
ORGANIZED RELIGION AND ORGANIZED CRIME
AshleighBrilliant.com
BOTH FLOURISH BECAUSE THEY SOMEHOW MEET SOCIETY'S NEEDS.

©ASHLEIGH BRILLIANT 2005. POT-SHOTS NO. 9791.

DON'T BE AFRAID ~
SHARE YOUR IDEAS ~

YOUR CANDLE
WON'T LOSE
ANY OF ITS BRIGHTNESS
BY LIGHTING OTHERS.

AshleighBrilliant.com

©ASHLEIGH BRILLIANT 2003. POT-SHOTS NO. 9293.

IT WOULD BE
FOOLISH
NOT TO HOPE
FOR THE BEST ~

BUT
EVEN MORE FOOLISH
TO EXPECT IT.

AshleighBrilliant.com

©ASHLEIGH BRILLIANT 1999. SANTA BARBARA. POT-SHOTS NO. 8243.

I DO EXPERIENCE
MOMENTS OF
VIVID REALITY ~

BUT FORTUNATELY, THEY SOON PASS.

www.AshleighBrilliant.com

©ASHLEIGH BRILLIANT 2003. POT-SHOTS NO. 9465.

WHEN TRUTH COMBATS ILLUSION,

TRUTH DOESN'T NECESSARILY ALWAYS WIN.

AshleighBrilliant.com

POT-SHOTS NO. 8312.
I ALWAYS CONSIDER EVERY POINT OF VIEW:
THAT'S WHY I CAN NEVER MAKE UP MY MIND.
www.AshleighBrilliant.com

©ASHLEIGH BRILLIANT 2005.
POT-SHOTS NO. 9683.
INTELLIGENT PEOPLE ASK HOW TO DO IT~
WISE PEOPLE ASK WHY IT NEEDS TO BE DONE.
AshleighBrilliant.com

©ASHLEIGH BRILLIANT 2001
POT-SHOTS NO. 8758.
WITHOUT GOD, THE WORLD DOESN'T MAKE SENSE
~ BUT THAT DOESN'T PROVE THAT THERE IS A GOD.
AshleighBrilliant.com

POT-SHOTS NO. 8752.

DON'T BE AFRAID TO FORGET ~

GOD KEEPS A COMPLETE RECORD OF EVERYTHING.

AshleighBrilliant.com

POT-SHOTS NO. 8327.

www.AshleighBrilliant.com

IF WE ALL UNDERSTOOD EVERYTHING,

THERE MIGHT BE NO POINT IN LIVING.

POT-SHOTS NO. 9598.

MY THEOLOGIAN SAYS THERE IS A GOD ~

BUT I FEEL I SHOULD GET A SECOND OPINION.

AshleighBrilliant.com

©ASHLEIGH BRILLIANT 1999. SANTA BARBARA. POT-SHOTS NO. 8346.

THE BEST THING ABOUT RELIGION

IS THAT WHILE PEOPLE ARE PRAYING, THEY CAN'T DO MUCH HARM.

www.AshleighBrilliant.com

©ASHLEIGH BRILLIANT 2003. POT-SHOTS NO. 9513.

LIFE NEED NOT BE AN EMPTY DREAM ~

IT CAN BE A VERY FULL ONE.

ashleighBrilliant.com

©ASHLEIGH BRILLIANT 1999. SANTA BARBARA. POT-SHOTS NO. 8618.

GOD IS A WONDERFUL ALLY ~

BUT HE REFUSES TO MAKE LONG-TERM COMMITMENTS.

www.AshleighBrilliant.com

©ASHLEIGH BRILLIANT 1999. SANTA BARBARA. POT-SHOTS NO. 8469.

ALL DISTANCE IS AN ILLUSION ~

IN REALITY, EVERYTHING TOUCHES EVERYTHING ELSE.

www.AshleighBrilliant.com

©ASHLEIGH BRILLIANT 1999. SANTA BARBARA POT-SHOTS NO. 8219.

PRAY ALL YOU LIKE ~

BUT IT'S ABSOLUTELY NO USE ASKING GOD TO BE REASONABLE.

©ASHLEIGH BRILLIANT 1999. SANTA BARBARA.
POT-SHOTS NO. 8604.
WHEN MY REAL PURPOSE IS FINALLY MADE KNOWN,
I HOPE I'LL BE THE FIRST TO BE INFORMED.
www.AshleighBrilliant.com

©ASHLEIGH BRILLIANT 1999. SANTA BARBARA.
POT-SHOTS NO. 8432.
www.AshleighBrilliant.com
YOU CAN NEVER LEAVE WHERE YOU ARE
BECAUSE WHERE YOU ARE IS ALWAYS WHERE YOU ARE.

©ASHLEIGH BRILLIANT 2003.
POT-SHOTS NO. 9536.
ANYONE WHO BELIEVES LIFE IS AN ILLUSION
OUGHT NOT TO BE TRUSTED WITH LARGE SUMS OF MONEY.
AshleighBrilliant.com

©ASHLEIGH BRILLIANT 2005. POT-SHOTS NO. 9986.

IF THINGS ARE NOT WHAT THEY SEEM,

WHAT ARE THEY?

AshleighBrilliant.com

©ASHLEIGH BRILLIANT 2005. POT-SHOTS NO. 9706.

MOST QUESTIONS HAVE ANSWERS ~

THE ONLY EXCEPTIONS ARE THE REALLY IMPORTANT ONES.

AshleighBrilliant.com

©ASHLEIGH BRILLIANT 1999. SANTA BARBARA. POT-SHOTS NO. 8451.

YOU CAN NEVER GET BELOW THE SURFACE OF REALITY ~

BECAUSE THE SURFACE GOES ALL THE WAY DOWN.

www.AshleighBrilliant.com

POT-SHOTS NO. 9972.

I HEAR THAT HELL IS VERY WELL-ORGANIZED.

AshleighBrilliant.com

4. Yours, Mine, and Hours

The human process of relating to each other is as variable time-wise as in every other respect. It may be as enduring as a life-long friendship, or as short-lived as a single dismal date. In actual fact, of course, all hours spent thus are equally long. But Time, in its role of Cosmic Magician, adeptly performs that well-known illusion of stretching misery and compressing happiness.

In any case, those tasty emotional entanglements which we call "relationships" tend to occur in a wide range of flavors, several of which you will find alluded to in this chapter. Most of these, including Friendship, involve communication via various media — but, when it comes to the medium called "Love," the observation that "the medium is the message" takes on all kinds of unexpected meanings. Fortunately, it is only in Tennis that "Love" means nothing.

The person-to-person messages which these epigrams embody need never, as demonstrated herein, exceed seventeen words in order to convey their full impact. But why did I decide on a maximum of seventeen? I've given other answers from time to time, but, just between us, I hope it may satisfy you to know that there happen to be exactly that many letters in my name.

© ASHLEIGH BRILLIANT 2003. POT-SHOTS NO. 9088.

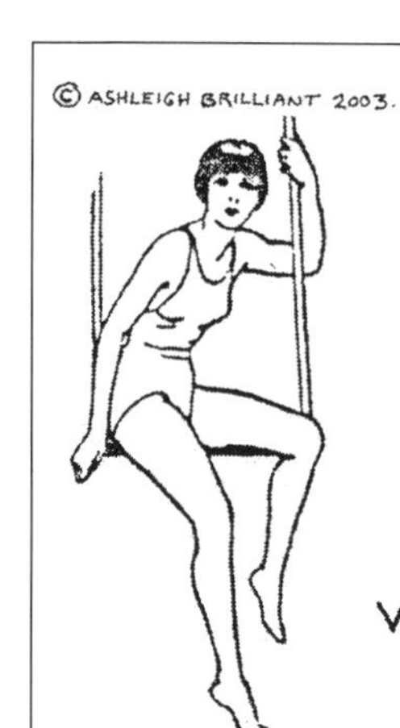

LOVE IS
A TRADE-OFF:

YOU GIVE
EVERYTHING,
AND YOU GET
WHATEVER YOU GET.

AshleighBrilliant.com

© ASHLEIGH BRILLIANT 2001 POT-SHOTS NO. 8785.

THOSE WHO THINK
CONVENTIONAL SEX
IS BETTER THAN
OTHER
KINDS

PROBABLY
HAVEN'T TRIED
MANY OTHER KINDS.

AshleighBrilliant.com

©ASHLEIGH BRILLIANT 1999. SANTA BARBARA. POT-SHOTS NO. 8345.

YOU MAY NOT HAVE EVERYTHING,

But at least you have me.

www.AshleighBrilliant.com

©ASHLEIGH BRILLIANT 2003. POT-SHOTS NO. 9326.

SOME OF MY FRIENDSHIPS ARE INSECURE ~

BUT IT'S VERY HARD TO BUY FRIENDSHIP INSURANCE.

AshleighBrilliant.com

©ASHLEIGH BRILLIANT 2005. POT-SHOTS NO. 9901.

WHETHER OR NOT YOU LOVE ME IS YOUR OWN AFFAIR ~

BUT I CAN'T HELP BEING CURIOUS.

AshleighBrilliant.com

©ASHLEIGH BRILLIANT 1999. SANTA BARBARA.
POT-SHOTS NO. 8446.
THE LANGUAGE OF LOVE
CAN BE LEARNED ONLY BY TOTAL IMMERSION.
www. Ashleigh Brilliant .com

©ASHLEIGH BRILLIANT 2005.
POT-SHOTS NO. 9313.
WHY CAN'T YOU REGARD MY CONSTANT NAGGING
AS A FORM OF ENCOURAGEMENT?
Ashleigh Brilliant .com

©ASHLEIGH BRILLIANT 2003.
POT-SHOTS NO. 9217.
THE MORE OF MY BEHAVIOR YOU ACCEPT,
THE LESS YOU WILL HAVE TO FORGIVE.
Ashleigh Brilliant.com

©ASHLEIGH BRILLIANT 2003.

POT-SHOTS NO. 9531.

THE EASIEST PEOPLE TO TALK TO

ARE THOSE WHO HAVE NOTHING ELSE TO DO.

AshleighBrilliant.com

©ASHLEIGH BRILLIANT 2003.
POT-SHOTS NO. 9175.
I WANT ALL THE
BAD PARTS OF YOU
OUT OF MY LIFE ~
(THE GOOD PARTS
CAN STAY).
ashleigh
Brilliant.com

©ASHLEIGH BRILLIANT 2005.
POT-SHOTS NO. 9849.
NEVER
FORGET
THAT I
LOVE YOU ~
AND DON'T
LET ME
FORGET IT EITHER.
ashleigh Brilliant.com

©ASHLEIGH BRILLIANT 1999. SANTA BARBARA.
POT-SHOTS NO. 8534.
DON'T
FEEL
NEGLECTED ~
IF I WERE
ALWAYS
WITH YOU,
WHAT
WOULD
YOU
HAVE
TO LOOK
FORWARD TO?
www.
ashleigh
Brilliant
.com

©ASHLEIGH BRILLIANT 2003. POT-SHOTS NO. 9543.

YOU HAVE MY LOVE~

WHY MUST YOU ALSO WANT MY RESPECT?

AshleighBrilliant.com

©ASHLEIGH BRILLIANT 1999. SANTA BARBARA. POT-SHOTS NO. 8593.

EVERY NEW DAY

MAY HAVE, SOMEWHERE IN IT, A NEW FRIEND, WAITING TO BE FOUND.

www.AshleighBrilliant.com

©ASHLEIGH BRILLIANT 1999. SANTA BARBARA.

POT-SHOTS NO. 8659.

FOR PEACE OF MIND,

YOU MUST FORGIVE WHAT YOU CAN'T FORGET,

AND FORGET WHAT YOU CAN'T FORGIVE.

www.AshleighBrilliant.com

©ASHLEIGH BRILLIANT 2003.

POT-SHOTS NO. 9565.

HOW MANY TIMES DO I HAVE TO TELL YOU

TO PAY NO ATTENTION TO ANYTHING I SAY?

AshleighBrilliant.com

©ASHLEIGH BRILLIANT 2003.

POT-SHOTS NO. 9522.

THE POWERFUL EFFECTS OF MEN UPON WOMEN

ARE EQUALLED ONLY BY THOSE OF WOMEN UPON MEN.

AshleighBrilliant.com

©ASHLEIGH BRILLIANT 2003.
POT-SHOTS NO. 9100.
SOMETIMES THE BEST WAY TO HELP SOMEONE
IS TO LET THAT PERSON HELP YOU.
ashleighbrilliant.com

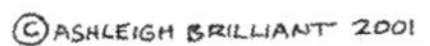

©ASHLEIGH BRILLIANT 2001
POT-SHOTS NO. 8694.
CIRCUMSTANCES BROUGHT US TOGETHER ~
But soon our love didn't need circumstances any more.
ashleighbrilliant.com

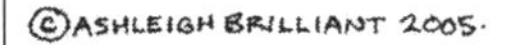

©ASHLEIGH BRILLIANT 2005.
POT-SHOTS NO. 9845.
ashleighbrilliant.com
I KNOW IT SOUNDS CRAZY ~
BUT THERE MAY BE SOME CONNECTION BETWEEN HAVING SEX AND HAVING BABIES.

POT-SHOTS NO. 8776.

LOVE HASN'T ALWAYS TIME

TO BE PROPER.

AshleighBrilliant.com

POT-SHOTS NO. 9612.

LET'S STAY ON GOOD TERMS ~

SOMEDAY WE MAY NEED EACH OTHER.

AshleighBrilliant.com

POT-SHOTS NO. 8805.

I RESPECT YOUR VALUES

BUT I DON'T SHARE THEM ~

— IN FACT, I DON'T EVEN UNDERSTAND THEM.

AshleighBrilliant.com

©ASHLEIGH BRILLIANT 2001
POT-SHOTS NO. 8899.
IF YOU ALWAYS DO WHAT'S MOST URGENT,
YOU MAY NEVER HAVE TIME FOR WHAT'S REALLY MOST IMPORTANT.
AshleighBrilliant.com

©ASHLEIGH BRILLIANT 2005.
POT-SHOTS NO. 9789.
IF YOU WANT TO STAY CONNECTED,
IT'S VERY IMPORTANT TO KEEP IN TOUCH.
AshleighBrilliant.com

©ASHLEIGH BRILLIANT 2001
POT-SHOTS NO. 8735.
NO SUCCESSFUL MARRIAGE
SHOULD REQUIRE AN INTERPRETER.
AshleighBrilliant.com

POT-SHOTS NO. 9740. ©ASHLEIGH BRILLIANT 2005.

LET'S NOT SPOIL OUR PRECIOUS TIME TOGETHER

BY TALKING ABOUT ANYTHING IMPORTANT.

AshleighBrilliant.com

©ASHLEIGH BRILLIANT 1999. SANTA BARBARA. POT-SHOTS NO. 8424.

LOVE IS A STRANGE COMMODITY,

BECAUSE YOU CAN'T IMPORT IT IF YOU DON'T ALSO EXPORT IT.

www.AshleighBrilliant.com

©ASHLEIGH BRILLIANT 2005. POT-SHOTS NO. 9724.

AshleighBrilliant.com

WHY DOES IT TAKE SO MUCH COURAGE

TO DEAL WITH THE PEOPLE I LOVE?

©ASHLEIGH BRILLIANT 2005. POT-SHOTS NO. 9842.

IN THE LONG RUN,

MARRIAGE IS BETTER THAN HAPPINESS.

AshleighBrilliant.com

©ASHLEIGH BRILLIANT 2003.
POT-SHOTS NO. 9186.
NOW PLAYING:
LIFE!
HURRY—
ENDS SOON!
ashleigh
Brilliant.com

©ASHLEIGH BRILLIANT 2001
POT-SHOTS NO. 8973.
IT'S
SURPRISING
HOW MUCH
OF MY PAST
IS STILL HIDING
IN THE PRESENT.
ashleigh
Brilliant.com

5. The Time of Your Life

In case you haven't noticed it lately, you are alive — which is more than can be said for all those who are not. The life-experience, as this chapter will demonstrate, is a fertile field for cogitation. No matter where you begin, thinking about life will take you along many a winding road — but don't expect any clearly legible sign-posts. The best you can hope for is to find friends along the way who are no less baffled than you are.

Nevertheless, the period between our arrival and departure, punctuated as it is with any number of inexplicables, is no time for panic or despair. With just one body and one mind at your disposal, you are entitled to consider simply keeping them in operation as convincing evidence of success.

Not that the task of being here and now is devoid of challenges. Every day, life is guaranteed to confront you with a day you have never experienced before. Whatever you make of it, or it makes of you, will be to some extent unprecedented and unrepeatable. In view of the vast range of opportunities life offers you, I can only say, thanks for choosing this moment to make my thoughts and my life a part of yours.

©ASHLEIGH BRILLIANT 2003.
POT-SHOTS NO. 9270.
HERE'S THE SITUATION:
I'M TRYING TO CHANGE THINGS,
WHILE THINGS ARE TRYING TO CHANGE ME.
ashleighbrilliant.com

©ASHLEIGH BRILLIANT 2005.
POT-SHOTS NO. 9921.
LIKE IT OR NOT,
WE HAVE TO STAY HERE ON EARTH,
UNTIL WE'RE RESCUED.
ashleighbrilliant.com

©ASHLEIGH BRILLIANT 2003.
POT-SHOTS NO. 9426.
WHEN YOU LEAVE A TRAIL OF KINDNESS,
HAPPINESS WILL ALWAYS KNOW WHERE TO FIND YOU.
ashleighbrilliant.com

POT-SHOTS NO. 9937.

THERE'S NO EXCUSE

FOR HAVING NO EXCUSE.

AshleighBrilliant.com

 POT-SHOTS NO. 8221.

I'LL NEVER GET USED TO LIVING AND DYING ~

NO MATTER HOW MANY TIMES I DO IT.

www.AshleighBrilliant.com

 POT-SHOTS NO. 9096.

ONLY BY GOING ON

CAN YOU ACQUIRE THE STRENGTH TO KEEP GOING ON.

AshleighBrilliant.com

©ASHLEIGH BRILLIANT 2005
POT-SHOTS NO. 9750.
YOU MAY NEVER KNOW WHAT YOU'RE ADDICTED TO,
UNTIL YOUR SUPPLY RUNS OUT.
ashleigh Brilliant.com

©ASHLEIGH BRILLIANT 2003
ashleigh Brilliant.com
POT-SHOTS NO. 9207.
FEWER PEOPLE HAVE REGRETS ABOUT THINGS THEY DID
THAN ABOUT THINGS THEY COULD HAVE DONE, BUT DIDN'T.

©ASHLEIGH BRILLIANT 2001
POT-SHOTS NO. 8953.
HOW COULD THERE POSSIBLY BE ANY MORE IMPORTANT PURPOSE IN LIFE
THAN HAVING FUN?
ashleigh Brilliant.com

©ASHLEIGH BRILLIANT 2003
POT-SHOTS NO. 9196.
THE PURPOSE OF LIFE
IS TO KEEP LIFE GOING UNTIL SOMEBODY FIGURES OUT ITS PURPOSE.
ashleighBrilliant.com

© ASHLEIGH BRILLIANT 2001
POT-SHOTS NO. 9009.
TWO OF THE STRANGEST PARTS OF LIFE
ARE COMING INTO IT
AND GOING OUT OF IT.
ashleigh Brilliant.com

POT-SHOTS NO. 9585. ©ASHLEIGH BRILLIANT 2003
WHY ISN'T THERE A PRIZE
FOR DOING THE LEAST HARM?
ashleighBrilliant.com

POT-SHOTS NO. 8922.

AshleighBrilliant.com

THEY SAY LIFE ALWAYS GOES ON ~

BUT THE ONLY ONES WHO SAY IT ARE THOSE STILL ALIVE.

POT-SHOTS NO. 9098.

HERE'S HOW TO MAKE LIFE EASIER:

KEEP LOWERING YOUR STANDARDS.

AshleighBrilliant.com

©ASHLEIGH BRILLIANT 2003. AshleighBrilliant.com POT-SHOTS NO. 9234.

YOU CAN ACCOMPLISH ALMOST ANYTHING,

IF YOU ARE SUFFICIENTLY BRAVE, CLEVER, AND UNSCRUPULOUS.

©ASHLEIGH BRILLIANT 2001 POT-SHOTS NO. 8905.

DON'T LET LIFE DEFEAT YOU!

SURRENDER TO IT IN ADVANCE.

AshleighBrilliant.com

©ASHLEIGH BRILLIANT 2003. AshleighBrilliant.com POT-SHOTS NO. 9517.

IF MORE OF US ARE LIVING LONGER,

IT MUST BE AT LEAST PARTLY BECAUSE WE WANT TO.

POT-SHOTS NO. 9289.

I EXPECTED TIMES LIKE THIS ~

BUT NEVER THOUGHT THEY'D BE SO BAD, SO LONG, AND SO FREQUENT.

ashleigh Brilliant.com

POT-SHOTS NO. 8800

SIMPLY AVOID KILLING YOURSELF,

AND YOU REDUCE YOUR RISK OF DEATH BY SUICIDE TO ZERO.

ashleigh Brilliant.com

POT-SHOTS NO. 9486.

ashleigh Brilliant.com

HOW CAN I BE SURE I'M READY,

UNLESS I KNOW WHAT I'M SUPPOSED TO BE READY FOR?

POT-SHOTS NO. 3592.

HOLD ON TO WHAT'S NECESSARY ~

LET GO OF WHAT'S NOT ~

AND WHEN IN DOUBT, LET GO.

©ASHLEIGH BRILLIANT 2003

AshleighBrilliant.com

I HAVE SOME WONDERFUL ANSWERS ~

DO YOU HAVE ANY INTERESTING QUESTIONS?

Ashleigh Brilliant.com

NO LAW REQUIRES PEOPLE TO BE POLITE AND CONSIDERATE,

EXCEPT THE LAW OF COMMON DECENCY.

www. Ashleigh Brilliant.com

LIFE IS NOT A MULTIPLE-CHOICE TEST ~

THE QUESTIONS DO NOT CONTAIN THE ANSWERS.

Ashleigh Brilliant.com

©ASHLEIGH BRILLIANT 2003. POT-SHOTS NO. 9449.

BIRTH AND DEATH ARE UNREPEATABLE EXPERIENCES ~

YOU HAVE TO GET THEM BOTH RIGHT THE FIRST TIME.

AshleighBrilliant.com

©ASHLEIGH BRILLIANT 1999. SANTA BARBARA POT-SHOTS NO. 8286.

LIFE BECOMES MORE PRECIOUS AS IT GETS SHORTER ~

BUT IT DOESN'T BECOME ANY MORE UNDERSTANDABLE.

www.AshleighBrilliant.com

©ASHLEIGH BRILLIANT 1999. SANTA BARBARA. POT-SHOTS NO. 8360.

OUR MERCHANDISE IS OVERPRICED,

BUT WORTH IT.

www.AshleighBrilliant.com

©ASHLEIGH BRILLIANT 2003. POT-SHOTS NO. 9341.

THE ADVANTAGE OF BEING DEAD

AshleighBrilliant.com

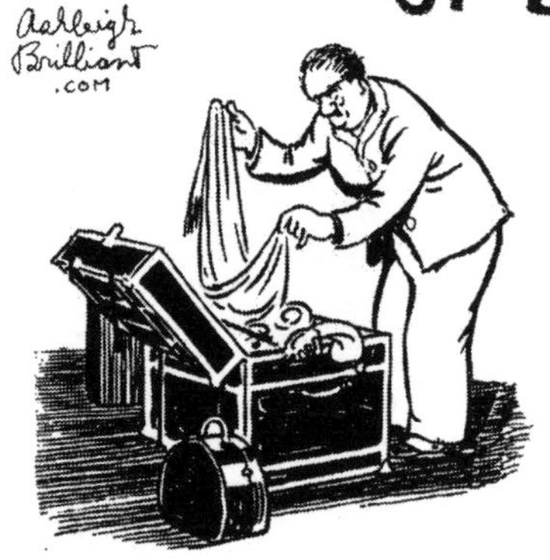

IS NOT HAVING TO SEE WHAT BECOMES OF EVERYTHING YOU LEFT BEHIND.

6. Time Is Money

Most of us, even though we're already alive, still have to make what is called "a living." As reflected in this chapter, some sort of "work" is usually involved — but the range of occupations can extend from the dramatic arts to the (somewhat related) art of politics, or from being a practiced criminal to practicing as a criminal attorney. One thing nearly all livelihoods have in common is that some form of compensation is provided for work performed. Emerson, in a famous Essay, looked upon the principle of Compensation as a kind of universal balancing act, regulating every aspect of life. Yet even in our technologically advanced society, the same idea usually comes down to a simple matter of payment by the hour or by the job.

Still, it cannot be denied that, upon this underpinning, vast new enterprises flourish. The surest indication of human activity is that money is changing hands (even if such exchanges are now even more "virtual" than they ever were, in the old days of metal, paper, and plastic.)

"Business," has come to mean much more than being busy— just as any discussion about the Economy will now have very little to do with being economical. We are often reminded that "Time is Money,"— but alas, money is not time. We don't know how much of it we have left, but we can't purchase a single instant more.

On the other hand, life can be very good while it lasts — and it's guaranteed to last your whole lifetime!

©ASHLEIGH BRILLIANT 2003. POT-SHOTS NO. 9553.

PEOPLE WHO ARE MORE INTERESTED IN THE WORK THAN IN THE MONEY

USUALLY MAKE MORE MONEY.

ashleigh Brilliant.com

IN WHICH ALL YOU HAVE IS A GOOD LEGAL CASE.

ashleigh Brilliant.com

©ASHLEIGH BRILLIANT 2001

WHY SHOULD
PRICES BE
THE SAME
FOR EVERYONE,

WHEN
SOME PEOPLE
HAVE
MORE MONEY
THAN OTHERS?

AshleighBrilliant.com

©ASHLEIGH BRILLIANT 2001 POT-SHOTS NO. 8756.

I DID ONCE HAVE A PERSONAL LIFE,

BUT I TRADED IT IN FOR A CAREER.

ashleigh Brilliant.com

©ASHLEIGH BRILLIANT 1999. SANTA BARBARA. POT-SHOTS NO. 8680.

A SURPLUS OF LAWYERS

DOES NOT NECESSARILY MEAN

AN ADEQUATE SUPPLY OF JUSTICE.

www.ashleigh Brilliant.com

©ASHLEIGH BRILLIANT 2003. POT-SHOTS NO. 9168.

SOME OF THE NICEST PEOPLE

MAKE A LIVING OUT OF OTHER PEOPLE'S MISFORTUNES.

AshleighBrilliant.com

©ASHLEIGH BRILLIANT 1999 POT-SHOTS NO. 8675.

NOBODY EVER GETS A CHANCE

TO MAKE MORE THAN ONE FATAL MISTAKE.

www.AshleighBrilliant.com SANTA BARBARA

©ASHLEIGH BRILLIANT 2001 POT-SHOTS NO. 8745.

DON'T ASK ME TO VOTE FOR YOU,

BECAUSE THE PEOPLE I VOTE FOR NEVER WIN.

AshleighBrilliant.com

POT-SHOTS NO. 8653.

MY WORK AND I
DEPEND ON EACH OTHER~

I KEEP
IT GOING,

AND IT
KEEPS
ME GOING.

www.AshleighBrilliant.com

POT-SHOTS NO. 9411.

ARE WEEKENDS
IN
HEAVEN

REALLY
WORTH
WEEKS
IN HELL?

AshleighBrilliant.com

POT-SHOTS NO. 8442.

THE MOST SUCCESSFUL
CRIMES

ARE
THE ONES
WE NEVER
HEAR ABOUT.

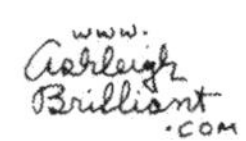

©ASHLEIGH BRILLIANT 1999. SANTA BARBARA.
POT-SHOTS NO. 8505.
IT TAKES LARGE GROUPS TO ACCOMPLISH MANY GREAT THINGS,
BUT NO CORPORATION HAS EVER WRITTEN A POEM.
www.AshleighBrilliant.com

©ASHLEIGH BRILLIANT 2003.
POT-SHOTS NO. 9197.
IT'S NOT SO BAD TO BE YOUR OWN BOSS ~
WHAT'S HARD IS TO BE YOUR OWN EMPLOYEE.
AshleighBrilliant.com

©ASHLEIGH BRILLIANT 2001
POT-SHOTS NO. 8704.
NEXT BEST TO ACTUALLY BEING RICH
IS BEING MISTAKENLY THOUGHT TO BE RICH.
AshleighBrilliant.com

 POT-SHOTS NO. 9580.

WHAT'S IMPORTANT

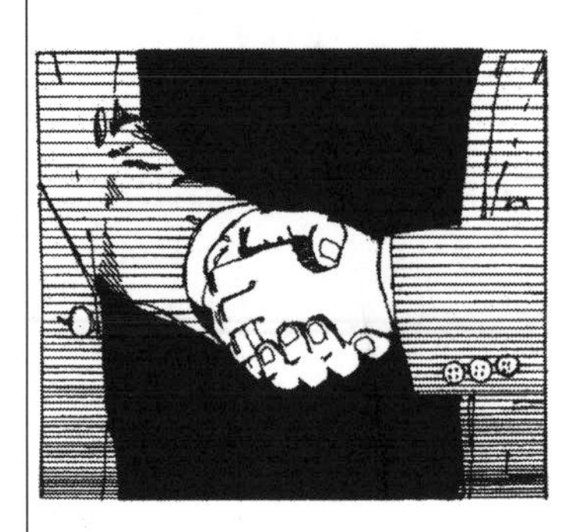

IS NOT
HOW MANY
PEOPLE
YOU KNOW,

BUT
HOW MANY
YOU CAN TRUST.

ashleighbrilliant.com

 POT-SHOTS NO. 8790.

ALL HONOR

ashleigh brilliant .com

TO THOSE
WHO DO
FOR MONEY

THE WORK
THAT NOBODY
REALLY
WANTS
TO DO.

 POT-SHOTS NO. 8769

MONEY
CAN
PERSUADE,

BUT HAS
NO ABILITY
TO TEACH.

ashleigh brilliant.com

POT-SHOTS NO. 8774.

WHY IS IT

THAT WHAT'S GOOD FOR LAWYERS

IS SELDOM GOOD FOR THE REST OF US?

AshleighBrilliant.com

POT-SHOTS NO. 9743.

BRIBERY

IS MUCH MORE CIVILIZED THAN INTIMIDATION,

AND, IN MOST CASES, IS ALL THAT'S NECESSARY.

AshleighBrilliant.com

POT-SHOTS NO. 9713.

I WANT FRIENDS,

BUT I HAVE NO OBJECTION IF THEY BEGIN AS CUSTOMERS.

AshleighBrilliant.com

©ASHLEIGH BRILLIANT 1999. SANTA BARBARA

POT-SHOTS NO. 8188.

WHY ARE CLEVER CRIMINALS SO RARE?

BECAUSE CLEVER PEOPLE CAN USUALLY MAKE A BETTER LIVING HONESTLY.

©ASHLEIGH BRILLIANT 2003.

POT-SHOTS NO. 9362.

YOUR CREDIT IS ALWAYS GOOD WITH ME

THAT'S WHY MY CREDIT ISN'T GOOD WITH ANYONE ELSE.

AshleighBrilliant.com

©ASHLEIGH BRILLIANT 1999. SANTA BARBARA.
POT-SHOTS NO. 8281.
ARGUMENTS CAN ALWAYS BE SETTLED,
IF BOTH SIDES GIVE A LITTLE,
OR ONE SIDE GIVES A LOT.
www.AshleighBrilliant.com

©ASHLEIGH BRILLIANT 2001
POT-SHOTS NO. 9002.
YIELDING BY ONE SIDE DOESN'T PROVE THE OTHER SIDE RIGHT,
BUT DOES AT LEAST SETTLE THE ISSUE.
AshleighBrilliant.com

©ASHLEIGH BRILLIANT 2003.
POT-SHOTS NO. 9368.
SORRY, WE CAN'T USE YOU ~
COME BACK WHEN YOU'VE SUFFERED SOME MORE.
AshleighBrilliant.com

POT-SHOTS NO. 9803.

IT COSTS MONEY TO MAKE MONEY ~

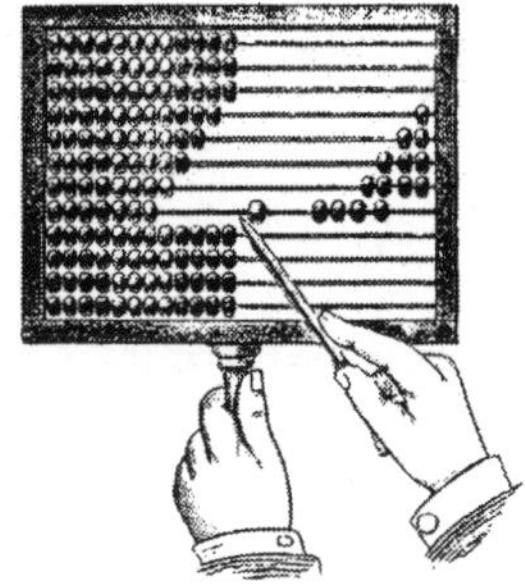

BUT IT'S NOT SUPPOSED TO COST MORE MONEY THAN YOU MAKE.

AshleighBrilliant.com

POT-SHOTS NO. 8429.

INFORMATION IS EASY TO GET ~

WHAT'S HARD TO GET IS UNDERSTANDING.

www.AshleighBrilliant.com

POT-SHOTS NO. 8503.

AVOID PEOPLE WHO PROMISE YOU EVERYTHING ~

UNLESS THEY ARE READY TO PAY A SUBSTANTIAL ADVANCE IN CASH.

www.AshleighBrilliant.com

©ASHLEIGH BRILLIANT 2003 POT-SHOTS NO. 9229.

NO MONTH GOES FASTER

THAN THE MONTH BETWEEN MY MONTHLY BILLS.

©ASHLEIGH BRILLIANT 2003. AshleighBrilliant.com POT-SHOTS NO. 9387

IF YOU OWE ME MONEY, PLEASE BE PROMPT ~

IF I OWE YOU MONEY, PLEASE BE PATIENT.

©ASHLEIGH BRILLIANT 2003.

POT-SHOTS NO. 9375.

AshleighBrilliant.com

HOW OLD YOU ARE

DOESN'T NECESSARILY DEPEND ON HOW LONG AGO YOU WERE BORN.

©ASHLEIGH BRILLIANT 2003.

POT-SHOTS NO. 9201.

THAT'S THE BEST WAY OF PUTTING IT BEHIND YOU.

AshleighBrilliant.com

7. Personal Time

You and I have at least one thing in common. We are "individuals,"— meaning we can't be divided. We are, each of us, a single irreducible unit, known as a "person." This is a big responsibility. But it also has certain advantages. Ultimately, nobody else is in command. Even when you're asleep, when that other part of you, the dreamer, takes over, whoever is in control is not anybody else. In sickness and in health, whether physical or mental, the person whom you call "I" or "Me" is the only one entirely and exclusively involved in your life.

What complicates things is that there are any number of other I's and Me's in circulation, all of whom are in the same predicament. Collectively they are known as "people," or "Humanity." You will find them almost everywhere — including this chapter. The question then arises, what is to be done about them? Some people will tell you, "Solitude is sweet." But others will counsel, "There is safety in numbers." This is known as "The Herd Instinct."

The wisest course is probably to seek some kind of solitude within the herd. That may be what dreams were made for.

POT-SHOTS NO. 9129.

THE GOOD THING ABOUT BEING ALONE

IS THAT YOU ALWAYS KNOW WHO'S IN CHARGE.

AshleighBrilliant.com

©ASHLEIGH BRILLIANT 1999. SANTA BARBARA.

POT-SHOTS NO. 8492.

THERE'S NO SHORT-CUT TO GOOD HEALTH ~

IN FACT, MOST SHORT-CUTS LEAD IN THE OPPOSITE DIRECTION.

www. AshleighBrilliant. com

©ASHLEIGH BRILLIANT 1999

POT-SHOTS NO. 8322.

IT'S EASIER PRETENDING I'M ASLEEP WHEN I'M REALLY AWAKE

THAN PRETENDING I'M AWAKE WHEN I'M REALLY ASLEEP.

www.AshleighBrilliant.com SANTA BARBARA

©ASHLEIGH BRILLIANT 2003.

POT-SHOTS NO. 9331.

PEOPLE WHO ACT AS IF NOTHING MATTERS

AshleighBrilliant.com

ARE USUALLY CONSIDERED INSANE

(ALTHOUGH THEY MAY ACTUALLY BE RIGHT.)

©ASHLEIGH BRILLIANT 2003.

POT-SHOTS NO. 9643.

WHEN YOUR BODY KEEPS SENDING YOU A MESSAGE,

VERY OFTEN THE MESSAGE IS: "I NEED A REST."

AshleighBrilliant.com

©ASHLEIGH BRILLIANT 2003. POT-SHOTS NO. 9384.

I DREAMED I HAD A GOOD LIFE ~

AT LEAST I HAD A GOOD DREAM.

AshleighBrilliant.com

©ASHLEIGH BRILLIANT 2003. POT-SHOTS NO. 9576.

NO MATTER HOW HARD I TRY,

I STILL CAN'T DO IT EFFORTLESSLY.

AshleighBrilliant.com

©ASHLEIGH BRILLIANT 1999. SANTA BARBARA. POT-SHOTS NO. 8331.

HERE'S HOW TO AVOID DISAPPOINTMENT:

LOWER YOUR EXPECTATIONS.

www.AshleighBrilliant.com

©ASHLEIGH BRILLIANT 2003.
POT-SHOTS NO. 9066.
THE RIGHT FOOD
IN THE
RIGHT AMOUNT
AT THE
RIGHT TIME
CAN BE
BETTER THAN
ANY DRUG.
ashleigh Brilliant.com

©ASHLEIGH BRILLIANT 1999. SANTA BARBARA
POT-SHOTS NO. 8371.
LOOK FOR ME
WHEREVER
THERE'S WORK
TO BE
AVOIDED
www.
ashleigh
Brilliant
.com

©ASHLEIGH BRILLIANT 1999. SANTA BARBARA.
POT-SHOTS NO. 8566.
www.
ashleigh
Brilliant
.com
WHY IS
WHAT GOES
INTO MY BODY
SO MUCH MORE
APPEALING
THAN
WHAT COMES
OUT OF IT?

©ASHLEIGH BRILLIANT 1999. SANTA BARBARA.
POT-SHOTS NO. 8473.
IF YOU DON'T BELIEVE IN IT,
YOU MAY NEVER FIND IT.
www.ashleighbrilliant.com

©ASHLEIGH BRILLIANT 2003.
POT-SHOTS NO. 9287.
OUR BEST REASON FOR TREATING CERTAIN ANIMALS WELL
IS THAT WE PLAN TO EAT THEM.
ashleighbrilliant.com

©ASHLEIGH BRILLIANT 1999. SANTA BARBARA.
POT-SHOTS NO. 8650.
WHAT'S THE GOOD OF HAVING PLENTY OF ENERGY,
IF THERE'S REALLY NOTHING I WANT TO DO?
www.ashleighbrilliant.com

©ASHLEIGH BRILLIANT 2003. ashleigh brilliant.com POT-SHOTS NO. 9245.

THE TROUBLE WITH WANTING TO DO NOTHING

IS THAT IT REQUIRES SO MUCH TIME.

©ASHLEIGH BRILLIANT 2001 POT-SHOTS NO. 8826.

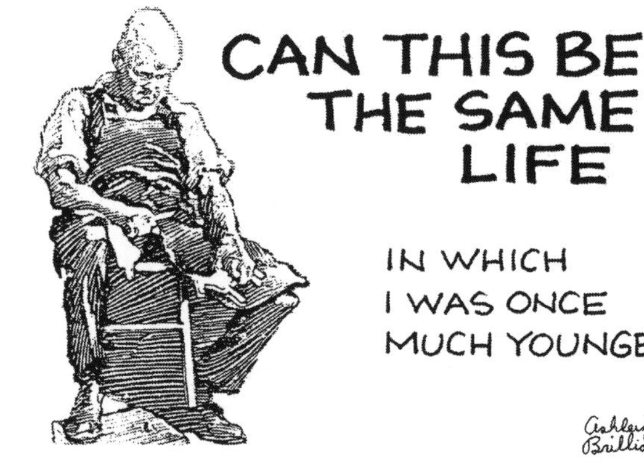

CAN THIS BE THE SAME LIFE

IN WHICH I WAS ONCE MUCH YOUNGER?

ashleigh brilliant.com

©ASHLEIGH BRILLIANT 2001 POT-SHOTS NO. 8827.

LAUGHTER AND WEEPING

BOTH BEGIN AT THE POINT WHERE REASON CAN GO NO FURTHER.

ashleigh brilliant.com

©ASHLEIGH BRILLIANT 2001

POT-SHOTS NO. 8739.

Ashleigh Brilliant .com

EVERY NIGHT,

MY DREAMS COME OUT IN A NEW EDITION.

©ASHLEIGH BRILLIANT 2005

POT-SHOTS NO. 9781.

WHY DOES WHAT'S BAD FOR YOU

SO OFTEN COST SO MUCH MORE

Ashleigh Brilliant.com

©ASHLEIGH BRILLIANT 2001 POT-SHOTS NO. 8917.

AshleighBrilliant.com

WAKING FROM MY DREAMS

ALWAYS SEEMS TO LEAVE A LOT OF UNFINISHED BUSINESS.

©ASHLEIGH BRILLIANT 2003 ashleighbrilliant.com POT-SHOTS NO. 9623.
IF MY MIND DIES BEFORE MY BODY
MUST I ATTEND THE FUNERAL?

©ASHLEIGH BRILLIANT 2001
POT-SHOTS NO. 9015.
WHO CAUSE MORE TROUBLE IN THE WORLD:
PEOPLE WITH TOO LITTLE SELF-ESTEEM,
OR PEOPLE WITH TOO MUCH?
ashleighbrilliant.com

©ASHLEIGH BRILLIANT 2003.
POT-SHOTS NO. 9297.
WHENEVER I THINK OF HER COOKING,
I GET A LUMP IN MY THROAT.
ashleighbrilliant.com

©ASHLEIGH BRILLIANT 1999. SANTA BARBARA.
POT-SHOTS NO. 8278.
WHAT RIGHT HAS ANYONE TO BE HAPPY,
IF I'M NOT?
www.AshleighBrilliant.com

©ASHLEIGH BRILLIANT 2001
POT-SHOTS NO. 8733.
I always celebrate the anniversary of my annual depression
by getting depressed.
AshleighBrilliant.com

8. Sooner or Later

Life is not a bed of roses. Indeed, unless all the thorns have been carefully removed, even a bed of roses may not be a bed of roses – if you know what I mean. And, no matter how well things may seem to be going at the moment, somehow, we are always able to find time for a little sadness, sickness, pain and trouble – to which the current chapter is more tearfully than cheerfully dedicated.

But you would hardly trust me to keep on having Brilliant Thoughts –would you? — if they were always optimistic and uplifting. Some of our difficulties may be based on incorrect information, some on disappointed hopes, some even on an overdose of reality. Modern medicine seems to have a pill for almost every ill, although some pills are still looking for their ills.

There are cases of people who make a regular practice of knocking their head against a brick wall "because it feels so good when I stop." It's hard to argue with that kind of logic – so I can only hope that, if you emerge unscathed from this chapter, you may, for a similar reason, feel at least a little better than when you went in.

POT-SHOTS NO. 8879.

WE'RE ALL CONDEMNED
TO SUFFERING,
STRUGGLE,
AND ULTIMATE
FUTILITY ~

Ashleigh Brilliant .com

TRY TO SEE
THE HUMOR
IN THIS SITUATION.

POT-SHOTS NO. 9473.

GOING...
GOING...

DECIDED
TO STAY.

Ashleigh Brilliant.com

POT-SHOTS NO. 8860.

WHY ARE
SO MANY PEOPLE
SO
UNNECESSARILY
AFRAID
OF SO MANY
THINGS?

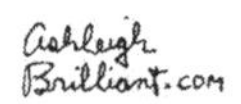

©ASHLEIGH BRILLIANT 1999. SANTA BARBARA.
POT-SHOTS NO. 8407.
I WANT NO PART IN ANY REAL TRAGEDY,
BUT I DON'T MIND BEING PART OF THE AUDIENCE.
www.AshleighBrilliant.com

©ASHLEIGH BRILLIANT 2003.
POT-SHOTS NO. 9467.
WHY DO WE PAY SO MUCH MORE FOR OUR MISTAKES
THAN WE ARE REWARDED FOR OUR EFFORTS?
AshleighBrilliant.com

©ASHLEIGH BRILLIANT 1999. SANTA BARBARA.
POT-SHOTS NO. 8421.
BAD EXPERIENCES CAN BE EVEN MORE VALUABLE THAN GOOD ONES
AND THEY CAN ALSO COST MUCH MORE.
www.AshleighBrilliant.com

©ASHLEIGH BRILLIANT 2001

POT-SHOTS NO. 8737.

WHY IS HELP

SO OFTEN MORE AVAILABLE WHEN IT'S NOT NEEDED THAN WHEN IT IS?

AshleighBrilliant.com

©ASHLEIGH BRILLIANT 2003.

POT-SHOTS NO. 9614.

POVERTY

IS ONLY ONE OF MANY CAREER OPTIONS NOW AVAILABLE.

AshleighBrilliant.com

©ASHLEIGH BRILLIANT 1999. SANTA BARBARA.

POT-SHOTS NO. 8478.

THERE'S NOTHING I CAN'T AFFORD~

SO LONG AS I PERMIT MYSELF TO GO DEEPLY INTO DEBT.

www.AshleighBrilliant.com

POT-SHOTS NO. 9551.

WHY DO
CERTAIN PAINS

SEEM TO
LIKE ME
SO MUCH?

AshleighBrilliant.com

POT-SHOTS NO. 8440.

EXACTLY
WHAT IS THE
PURPOSE

OF
UNCOMFORTABLE
WEATHER?

www.
AshleighBrilliant.com

POT-SHOTS NO. 9028.

I HOPE
YOU'RE NOT
GETTING
TOO MUCH
PLEASURE
OUT OF
BEING
SICK.

AshleighBrilliant.com

©ASHLEIGH BRILLIANT 2003.
POT-SHOTS NO. 9651.
SOMETIMES
THE ONLY HELP
ANYONE
CAN PROVIDE
IS JUST
TO BE
BESIDE YOU
IN YOUR TROUBLE.
ashleighBrilliant.com

© ASHLEIGH BRILLIANT 2001
POT-SHOTS
NO. 8836.
OF COURSE I'M
DEALING
WITH THE
PROBLEM:
BY
REFUSING
TO TALK
OR THINK
ABOUT IT.
ashleigh
Brilliant.com

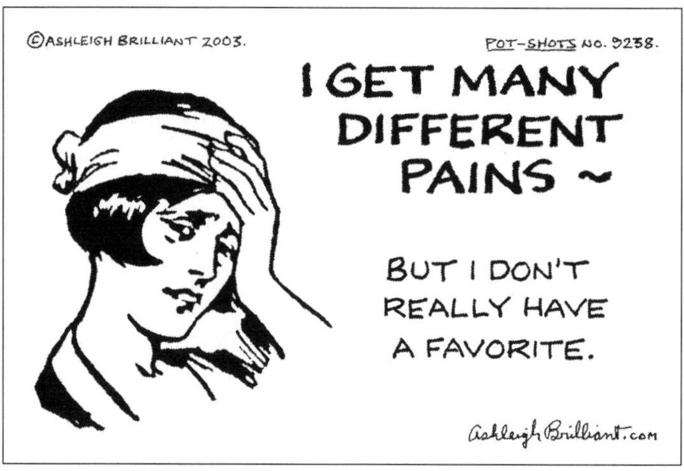
©ASHLEIGH BRILLIANT 2003.
POT-SHOTS NO. 9238.
I GET MANY
DIFFERENT
PAINS ~
BUT I DON'T
REALLY HAVE
A FAVORITE.
ashleighBrilliant.com

POT-SHOTS NO. 9254.

MANY
PEOPLE
NEED
LESSONS

IN
HOW TO BE
NICER TO ME.

AshleighBrilliant.com

POT-SHOTS NO. 9662.

ANY LAW
WHICH PROTECTS
ANYONE'S RIGHT
TO DO
BAD THINGS

IS A
BAD LAW.

AshleighBrilliant.com

POT-SHOTS NO. 8404.

WHAT WE CALL
COURAGE

IS OFTEN
SIMPLY
A FAILURE
TO UNDERSTAND
THE ODDS.

www.AshleighBrilliant.com

©ASHLEIGH BRILLIANT 1999. SANTA BARBARA.

POT-SHOTS NO. 8683.

POVERTY
IS NO CRIME
AND NO SIN,

BUT
CAN SOMETIMES BE
A SERIOUS
INCONVENIENCE.

www.AshleighBrilliant.com

©ASHLEIGH BRILLIANT 2003

POT-SHOTS NO. 9272.

AshleighBrilliant.com

PAIN
AND GARBAGE
ARE BOTH
UNWANTED ~

BUT
FOR SOME REASON,
PAIN
IS MUCH HARDER
TO THROW AWAY.

©ASHLEIGH BRILLIANT 2005.

POT-SHOTS NO. 9814.

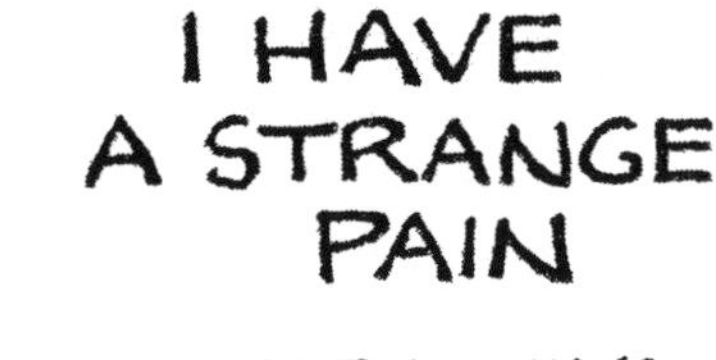

THAT ALWAYS
GOES
WHEN YOU COME,
AND COMES
WHEN YOU GO.

ashleighBrilliant.com

©ASHLEIGH BRILLIANT 2005. POT-SHOTS NO. 9773.

IT WAS HORRIBLE!

ONE MINUTE,
MY ILLUSIONS
WERE THERE —
THE NEXT,
THEY WERE GONE!

AshleighBrilliant.com

©ASHLEIGH BRILLIANT 2003. POT-SHOTS NO. 9454.

THE ONLY THING WE HAVE TO FEAR

IS PAIN, DEATH, LOSS, SICKNESS, AND PUBLIC SPEAKING.

AshleighBrilliant.com

©ASHLEIGH BRILLIANT 2001 POT-SHOTS NO. 8696.

WHAT I WANT

IS A COUNSELOR WHO WILL ACCEPT SOME PERSONAL RESPONSIBILITY FOR ALL MY PROBLEMS.

AshleighBrilliant.com

©ASHLEIGH BRILLIANT 2001

POT-SHOTS NO. 8998.

WHEN YOUR WORLD COMES APART,

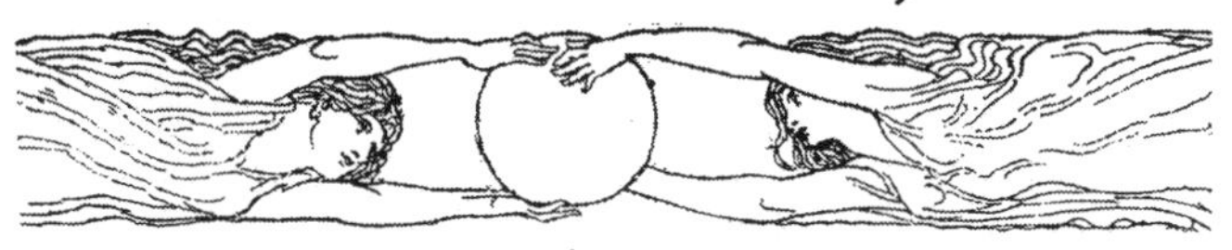

you must put it back together, or somehow find a new one.

AshleighBrilliant.com

POT-SHOTS NO. 8467.

MY MOST RIGID PRINCIPLE IS:

ALWAYS BE FLEXIBLE.

www.AshleighBrilliant.com

POT-SHOTS NO. 9117.

ALL WE NEED FOR A PEACEFUL WORLD

IS TO BAN ALL DISCUSSION OF POLITICS, SEX, AND RELIGION.

ashleighBrilliant.com

9. World Enough and Time

Occasionally the world demands to be taken seriously, even though we know it is all a big joke, featuring wars, governments, criminals, and any number of other hilarious ingredients to tickle our sense of the ludicrous.

Of course, we are dimly aware that ours is not the only world — but it is sufficient for most practical purposes. And "World Affairs," as they are called, need hardly take account of any activities beyond the range of our familiar news agencies. Even within that relatively narrow compass, however, things are going on which can scarcely be characterized as edifying. The question then arises as to whether we should take the world as we find it, and leave it to its own devices — or whether we have some sort of obligation to intervene.

Perhaps the answer is that we need inducements or incentives to "do the right thing." Undoubtedly there are vast areas capable of improvement, even in what some philosophers used to insist is "the best of all possible worlds." But still, it might be argued that, just as forest fires provide fertile space for new growth, an occasional mega-war on Planet Earth helps to clear the air (at least, once the radioactivity has dissipated.)

©ASHLEIGH BRILLIANT 2001

POT-SHOTS NO. 8692.

IF IT'S A RACE BETWEEN CIVILIZATION AND EXTINCTION,

MY HEART'S WITH CIVILIZATION,

BUT MY MONEY'S ON EXTINCTION.

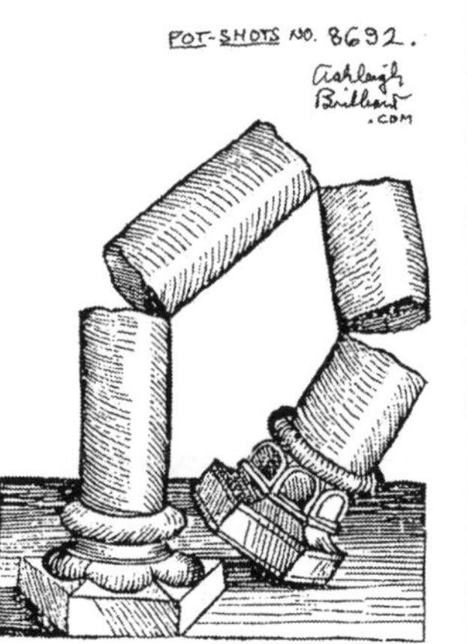

POT-SHOTS NO. 8382.

SURPRISINGLY OFTEN,

THE PEOPLE WHO WIN A WAR

DON'T GET WHAT THEY THOUGHT THEY WERE FIGHTING FOR.

www.AshleighBrilliant.com

POT-SHOTS NO. 9827.

IS MORNING REALLY A NEW BEGINNING,

OR JUST ANOTHER TURN OF THE SAME OLD PLANET?

AshleighBrilliant.com

©ASHLEIGH BRILLIANT 1999. SANTA BARBARA.
POT-SHOTS NO. 8310.
THE WAR'S BEEN OVER A LONG TIME ~
BUT IT'S STILL TOO EARLY TO SAY WHO REALLY WON.
www.ashleighbrilliant.com

© ASHLEIGH BRILLIANT 2003.
POT-SHOTS NO. 9338.
IF YOU WON'T DO IT FOR ME BECAUSE IT'S SHAMEFUL AND BARBARIC,
DO IT FOR YOUR COUNTRY.
ashleighbrilliant.com

©ASHLEIGH BRILLIANT 1999. SANTA BARBARA.
POT-SHOTS NO. 8398.
HOW CAN I MAKE ANY PLANS,
IF THE PEOPLE MY PLANS DEPEND ON KEEP CHANGING THEIRS?
www.ashleighbrilliant.com

©ASHLEIGH BRILLIANT 2005
POT-SHOTS NO. 9822.
Many things still exist only because
they would cost too much to get rid of.
AshleighBrilliant.com

©ASHLEIGH BRILLIANT 2003.
POT-SHOTS NO. 9126.
WHY SHOULD MAJORITIES RULE,
WHEN THEY ARE SO OFTEN WRONG?
AshleighBrilliant.com

©ASHLEIGH BRILLIANT 1999. SANTA BARBARA.
POT-SHOTS NO. 8299.
WHY ARE SO MANY PEOPLE IN POSITIONS OF AUTHORITY
OBVIOUSLY TIRED, BORED, AND INCOMPETENT?
www.AshleighBrilliant.com

POT-SHOTS NO. 8229.

NOTHING HAPPENING
IN THE WORLD TODAY
NEED TROUBLE YOU~

NOT UNLESS
YOU'RE A
THINKING, FEELING
HUMAN BEING.

www.AshleighBrilliant.com

©ASHLEIGH BRILLIANT 2003.
POT-SHOTS NO. 9370.
DIDN'T YOU BRING ANYTHING BACK FROM THE WAR,
APART FROM THAT LOOK IN YOUR EYE?
ashleigh Brilliant .com

©ASHLEIGH BRILLIANT 1999. SANTA BARBARA.
POT-SHOTS NO. 8236.
SOMETIMES IT TAKES AN OUTSIDER
TO SEE WHAT SHOULD HAVE BEEN OBVIOUS TO THOSE INSIDE.
www. ashleigh Brilliant .com

©ASHLEIGH BRILLIANT 2003.
POT-SHOTS NO. 9336.
MY MISSION ON EARTH IS SO SECRET,
THEY HAVEN'T YET TOLD ME WHAT IT IS.
ashleighBrilliant.com

©ASHLEIGH BRILLIANT 1999. SANTA BARBARA. POT-SHOTS NO. 8552.

CELIBATE PEOPLE DON'T LIVE LONGER THAN OTHERS ~

IT JUST SEEMS LONGER.

www.AshleighBrilliant.com

©ASHLEIGH BRILLIANT 2003. POT-SHOTS NO. 9466.

"DIE FOR THIS SACRED CAUSE!"

"WHAT MAKES IT SACRED?"

"ALL THOSE WHO'VE ALREADY DIED FOR IT."

AshleighBrilliant.com

©ASHLEIGH BRILLIANT 2001 POT-SHOTS NO. 8748.

WHY WOULD ANYONE WANT TO LIVE

IN MOST OF THE PLACES WHERE MOST PEOPLE ACTUALLY DO LIVE?

AshleighBrilliant.com

©ASHLEIGH BRILLIANT 2003 POT-SHOTS NO. 9081.

TRUST ME:

THAT'S AN ORDER!

AshleighBrilliant.com

©ASHLEIGH BRILLIANT 2003. ashleigh Brilliant.com POT-SHOTS NO. 9537.

SOMETIMES WAR INDICATES A FAILURE OF DIPLOMACY ~

SOMETIMES DIPLOMACY INDICATES A FAILURE OF WAR.

©ASHLEIGH BRILLIANT 2003. POT-SHOTS NO. 9046

I AM WILLING TO ACCEPT THE CONSEQUENCES OF MY ACTIONS ~

ESPECIALLY THE GOOD ONES.

ashleigh Brilliant.com

©ASHLEIGH BRILLIANT 2001

POT-SHOTS NO. 8792.

NEXT TIME WE'RE TOGETHER,

LET'S TRY TO KEEP THE VIOLENCE TO A MINIMUM.

AshleighBrilliant.com

©ASHLEIGH BRILLIANT 2005.

POT-SHOTS NO. 9719.

I CHALLENGED MYSELF TO A FIGHT~

BUT AT THE APPOINTED TIME, I FAILED TO APPEAR.

AshleighBrilliant.com

©ASHLEIGH BRILLIANT 2003.

POT-SHOTS NO. 9246

AshleighBrilliant.com

I REMEMBER GOOD AND EVIL WERE IN A BIG STRUGGLE~

BUT I NEVER HEARD THE FINAL RESULT.

POT-SHOTS NO. 8795.

AshleighBrilliant.com

I'M GLAD I DON'T HAVE TO BE HAPPY EVERY DAY ~

THE STRAIN MIGHT SERIOUSLY DAMAGE MY HEALTH.

POT-SHOTS NO. 9595.

THE HARDEST SACRIFICE OF ALL:

GIVING UP ABSTINENCE.

AshleighBrilliant.com

10. Trying Times

Nobody wants trouble; but some of us get more than our fair share — and it never seems to come at the right time. Suffer with me, then, through this chapter. Better times (or at least more cheerful chapters) are coming. In the meantime, let us remember the comforting maxim that a trouble shared is a trouble doubled. In the field of Human Relations alone, there is more than enough scope for misery in one's relations with oneself, before venturing out to relate to other people and their troubles.

Where those others are concerned, conflict seems to be the name of the game (which is fortunate for writers of fiction and drama, who'd be lost without it.) But avoiding conflict may be another recipe for loneliness, of which too many concoctions are already floating around. Far better, perhaps, to sally forth waving the brave banner of "Come What May!" The trouble is that this obligates you to deal with whatever may come.

But if you are seeking variety (or even if you're not) life offers more than one way of being unhappy, no matter what anguish you speak. So, without further ado, I trust you'll find herein something negative that you can relate to.

©ASHLEIGH BRILLIANT 1999. SANTA BARBARA
POT-SHOTS NO. 8181.
SHALL WE TALK FIRST, AND THEN FIGHT,
OR FIGHT FIRST, AND THEN TALK?
www.AshleighBrilliant.com

©ASHLEIGH BRILLIANT 2001
POT-SHOTS NO. 8781.
THERE'S NO LAW AGAINST BEHAVING STRANGELY~
BUT DON'T BE SURPRISED IF IT GETS YOU INTO TROUBLE.
AshleighBrilliant.com

©ASHLEIGH BRILLIANT 2005.
POT-SHOTS NO. 9914.
THE HARDEST PARTS OF LIVING, FOR ME,
ARE THE DAYS AND THE NIGHTS.
AshleighBrilliant.com

©ASHLEIGH BRILLIANT 1999. SANTA BARBARA. POT-SHOTS NO. 8644.

BEING UNHAPPY AT HOME

IS AT LEAST
USUALLY MORE COMFORTABLE
THAN BEING UNHAPPY
SOMEWHERE ELSE.

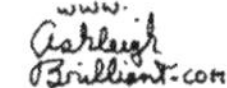

©ASHLEIGH BRILLIANT 2005.
POT-SHOTS NO. 9995.
NO MATTER HOW MANY THINGS I LOVE,
IT ALWAYS HURTS TERRIBLY TO LOSE EVEN ONE OF THEM.
Ashleigh Brilliant .com

© ASHLEIGH BRILLIANT 2005.
POT-SHOTS NO. 9857.
STUPIDITY
IS ITS OWN EXCUSE.
Ashleigh Brilliant .com

©ASHLEIGH BRILLIANT 1999. SANTA BARBARA.
POT-SHOTS NO. 8168
SOMEBODY SHOULD DO SOMETHING
ABOUT WHAT ONLY I CAN DO ANYTHING ABOUT.
www.AshleighBrilliant.com

©ASHLEIGH BRILLIANT 2003.
POT-SHOTS NO. 9491.
A GOOD REASON TO STAY AWAY FROM HOME
IS THAT HOME IS WHERE MOST ACCIDENTS HAPPEN.
ashleigh Brilliant .com

©ASHLEIGH BRILLIANT 1999. SANTA BARBARA
POT-SHOTS NO. 8179.
www. ashleigh Brilliant .com
I'VE TRIED PERSUASION ~
I'VE TRIED FORCE ~
BUT I STILL CAN'T MAKE PEOPLE LOVE ME.

©ASHLEIGH BRILLIANT 2003.
POT-SHOTS NO. 9133.
ONCE AGAIN, THE MEDIA HAVE MADE THE COURAGEOUS DECISION
TO PANDER TO THE PUBLIC'S BASEST INSTINCTS.
ashleighBrilliant.com

POT-SHOTS NO. 9527.

I DIDN'T LOSE INTEREST IN YOU ~

I JUST GOT SCARED.

ashleigh Brilliant.com

POT-SHOTS NO 9109.

IF YOU WANT TO MAKE PROGRESS,

THE FIRST STEP IS TO GET OUT OF YOUR OWN WAY.

ashleigh Brilliant.com

POT-SHOTS NO. 9685.

IF WE WERE TOTALLY PREPARED FOR EVERY DISASTER,

WHAT WOULD BE THE POINT OF HAVING DISASTERS?

ashleigh Brilliant.com

© ASHLEIGH BRILLIANT 2003. POT-SHOTS NO. 9318.

LIFE ISN'T EASY ~

AND LITTLE CHILDREN HAVE TO FACE MORE YEARS OF IT THAN ANYONE ELSE.

AshleighBrilliant.com

© ASHLEIGH BRILLIANT 1999. SANTA BARBARA. POT-SHOTS NO. 8324.

THERE'S NO WAY TO BREAK OUT OF THE HERE AND NOW:

WE'RE ALL TRAPPED IN IT FOREVER.

www.AshleighBrilliant.com

© ASHLEIGH BRILLIANT 2001 POT-SHOTS NO. 8952.

SHOULD I BLAME MYSELF FOR EVER GETTING INVOLVED WITH YOU ~

OR WAS IT AN HONEST MISTAKE?

AshleighBrilliant.com

©ASHLEIGH BRILLIANT 2003.
POT-SHOTS NO. 9181.
THERE YOU GO AGAIN ~
MAKING SENSE.
ashleigh Brilliant.com

©ASHLEIGH BRILLIANT 2001
POT-SHOTS NO. 8984.
WHEN YOU DON'T HAVE TROUBLE,
SOMEHOW YOU DON'T MISS IT.
ashleigh Brilliant.com

©ASHLEIGH BRILLIANT 2005.
POT-SHOTS NO. 9709.
WE MUST BE GETTING NEAR CIVILIZATION ~
LOOK AT ALL THE PRISONS!
ashleigh Brilliant.com

POT-SHOTS NO. 9024.

Ashleigh Brilliant.com

ANYONE
WHO ATTEMPTS
TO DISPROVE
MY CONSPIRACY
THEORY

IS OBVIOUSLY
PART OF
THE CONSPIRACY.

POT-SHOTS NO. 9281.

SOMETIMES
IT'S EASIER
TO BE
BELIEVED,

IF
YOU DON'T
TELL
THE TRUTH.

AshleighBrilliant.com

POT-SHOTS NO. 9973.

DOING
NOTHING

MAY BE
THE BIGGEST RISK
YOU CAN TAKE.

AshleighBrilliant.com

POT-SHOTS NO. 9073.

NOTHING COMES WITH MORE HIDDEN COSTS

THAN A WIFE.

AshleighBrilliant.com

POT-SHOTS NO. 9139.

WHEN I'M FREE, I WISH I WERE BUSY ~

AND WHEN I'M BUSY, I WISH I WERE FREE.

AshleighBrilliant.com

POT-SHOTS NO. 9855

IT ISN'T VERY COMFORTABLE,

LIVING IN THE RUINS OF A RELATIONSHIP.

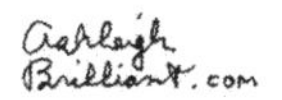

POT-SHOTS NO. 9080.

HOW CAN I GET THE RESULTS I WANT,

WITHOUT ALSO GETTING THE CONSEQUENCES I DON'T WANT?

ashleighbrilliant.com

POT-SHOTS NO. 9929.

ashleighbrilliant.com

DOCTORS CAN'T MAKE YOU IMMORTAL ~

BUT, WITH GOOD LUCK, THEY CAN PROLONG YOUR SUFFERING INDEFINITELY.

POT-SHOTS NO. 9483.

WHY SHOULD I PAY FOR TROUBLE AND ANNOYANCE,

WHEN SO MUCH IS AVAILABLE FREE OF CHARGE?

ashleighbrilliant.com

©ASHLEIGH BRILLIANT 2001
POT-SHOTS NO. 8759.
DO I WANT TO KNOW THE TRUTH?
~ THAT DEPENDS ON WHAT IT IS.
AshleighBrilliant.com

©ASHLEIGH BRILLIANT 2005.
POT-SHOTS NO. 9866.
AshleighBrilliant.com
WITH MODERN COMMUNICATIONS,
WE CAN BE CLOSER TO PEOPLE FAR AWAY
THAN TO THOSE NEARBY.

11. Time Out of Mind

Warning: Big Ideas Ahead! But they're never expressed in more than seventeen words, so your mind should be able to wrap itself snugly around them. Here you will find thoughtful discussion of many subjects you may never have thought to discuss, from the incredible to the inedible.

The truth is that nobody really knows what the truth is — and that, in itself, should be a very comforting thought. There are indeed certain laws of nature, which everyone believed to be fixed and immutable — until Einstein, and others of his ilk, came along and called everything into question. But what's truly surprising is how little any of this affects you and me in our daily lives. Only when abstract science comes down to the level of useful technology — a process which may take several centuries — are we likely to stop yawning, and reach for our credit-cards.

Nevertheless, the shreds of true knowledge at which we grasp, whether relating to inner or outer space, to the human world or to the world of "nature," remain elusive, and far from conclusive. When all is said and done about our role in the Cosmos, a great deal has been said, but very little has been done. In the end it all comes down to one eternally unanswered question:

"What's the Big Idea?"

©ASHLEIGH BRILLIANT 2003.
POT-SHOTS NO. 9052.
YOU CAN DECIDE TO STUDY IT ~
BUT YOU CAN'T DECIDE TO UNDERSTAND IT.
AshleighBrilliant.com

©ASHLEIGH BRILLIANT 2003.
POT-SHOTS NO. 9558.
WHERE THERE ARE NO PEOPLE,
NOTHING IS GOOD OR BAD.
AshleighBrilliant.com

©ASHLEIGH BRILLIANT 2005.
POT-SHOTS NO. 9694.
THE PURPOSE OF MACHINES IS TO MAKE US HAPPY ~
IF THEY DON'T, IT'S OUR FAULT, NOT THEIRS.
AshleighBrilliant.com

POT-SHOTS NO. 9873.

THERE'S NO WAY OUT ~

WE HAVE TO STAY IN THE UNIVERSE FOREVER

(IN SOME FORM OR OTHER).

AshleighBrilliant.com

POT-SHOTS NO. 8963.

AshleighBrilliant.com

MANY THINGS IN JUNKYARDS BELONG IN ART GALLERIES ~

AND MANY THINGS IN ART GALLERIES BELONG IN JUNKYARDS.

POT-SHOTS NO. 9269.

AshleighBrilliant.com

©ASHLEIGH BRILLIANT 2003.
POT-SHOTS NO. 9476.
WHY ISN'T MORE BEING DONE
TO PREVENT CRUELTY TO ANIMALS
BY OTHER ANIMALS?
ashleigh Brilliant .com

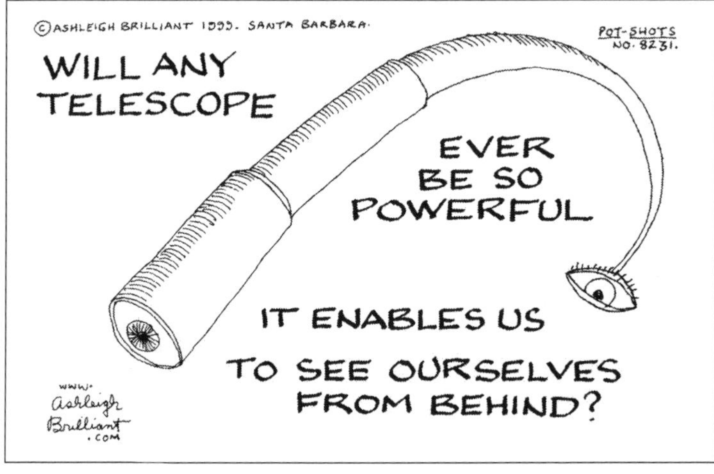
©ASHLEIGH BRILLIANT 1999. SANTA BARBARA.
POT-SHOTS NO. 8231.
WILL ANY TELESCOPE
EVER BE SO POWERFUL
IT ENABLES US
TO SEE OURSELVES FROM BEHIND?
www. ashleigh Brilliant .com

©ASHLEIGH BRILLIANT 2003. ashleighBrilliant.com
POT-SHOTS NO. 9334.
CAN THIS GALAXY BE SAVED?
IF NOT, DOES IT REALLY MATTER, WHEN THERE ARE SO MANY OTHERS?

©ASHLEIGH BRILLIANT 2003.
POT-SHOTS NO. 9086.
DOES TECHNOLOGY REALLY IMPROVE MY LIFE ~
OR JUST MAKE IT MORE COMPLICATED?
ashleighbrilliant.com

©ASHLEIGH BRILLIANT 2005.
POT-SHOTS NO. 9703.
WHEN ALL OUR BRAINS CONNECT INTO ONE BIG MIND,
WHO WILL DECIDE WHAT IT THINKS ABOUT?
ashleighbrilliant.com

©ASHLEIGH BRILLIANT 2003.
POT-SHOTS NO. 9402.
JUST BECAUSE YOU'RE NECESSARY
DOESN'T MEAN YOU'RE IMPORTANT.
ashleighbrilliant.com

©ASHLEIGH BRILLIANT 2001
POT-SHOTS NO. 8788.
THE
TRUE GENIUS
OF A
CIVILIZATION
LIES
NOT IN ITS
LITERATURE,
BUT IN
ITS PLUMBING.
ashleighBrilliant.com

©ASHLEIGH BRILLIANT 1999 SANTA BARBARA.
POT-SHOTS NO. 8356.
Well,
at least I can
cross Earth off
my list of
planets
I haven't
yet
visited.
www.ashleigh
Brilliant.com

POT-SHOTS NO. 9754.
WATER
IS NEVER
TOO DEEP
TO FLOAT ON.
©ASHLEIGH BRILLIANT 2005.
ashleighBrilliant.com

POT-SHOTS NO. 8245.

IN NATURE,

THE STRONGEST
AND
THE FASTEST

ALWAYS
HAVE THE
RIGHT OF WAY.

www.AshleighBrilliant.com

POT-SHOTS NO. 9239.

PEACE
AND
QUIET

IS A
PRECIOUS
NATURAL
RESOURCE,

which as yet, however,
cannot be transported.

AshleighBrilliant.com

©ASHLEIGH BRILLIANT 1999. SANTA BARBARA.

POT-SHOTS NO. 8663.

BETWEEN
THE INFINITE BEYOND US

AND THE INFINITE
WITHIN US,

THERE'S A
VERY STRANGE THING
CALLED "US."

www.AshleighBrilliant.com

ASHLEIGH BRILLIANT 2003.

POT-SHOTS NO. 9203.

WHEN CIRCLES
WERE INVENTED,

WHY
DIDN'T THEY
MAKE THE
CIRCUMFERENCE
EXACTLY
THREE TIMES
BIGGER THAN
THE DIAMETER?

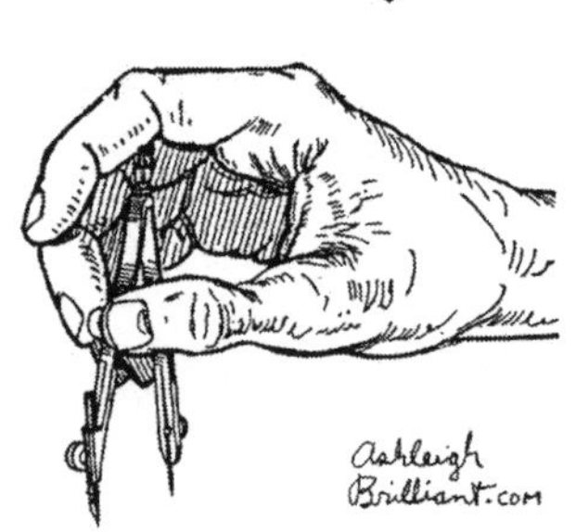

AshleighBrilliant.com

©ASHLEIGH BRILLIANT 2001

POT-SHOTS NO. 8719.

SCIENCE
IS A PROCESS OF
GIVING THINGS
NAMES,

AND FINDING
NEW THINGS
TO GIVE NAMES TO.

AshleighBrilliant.com

©ASHLEIGH BRILLIANT 2003.
POT-SHOTS NO. 9211.
EVERYTHING POSSIBLE IS BEING DONE
ashleigh Brilliant .com
TO OBSCURE THE FACT THAT WE REALLY DON'T KNOW WHAT TO DO.

©ASHLEIGH BRILLIANT 2001
POT-SHOTS NO. 8716.
IT TAKES ORGANIZATION AND DETERMINATION
TO DO MOST OF THE THINGS WHICH I WILL PROBABLY NEVER DO.
ashleigh Brilliant.com

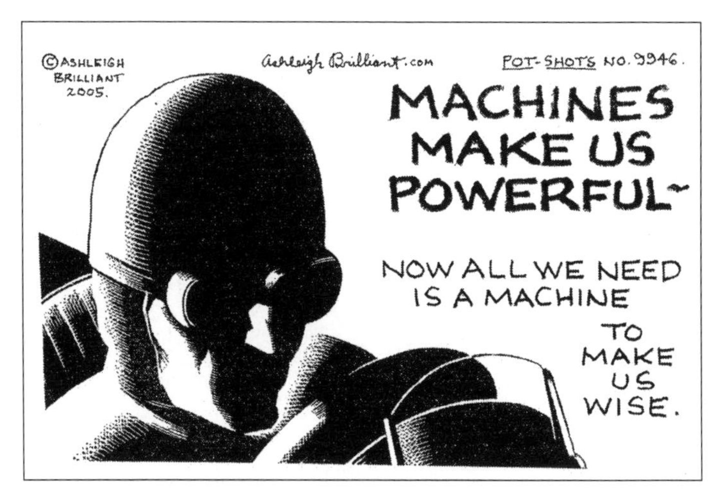
©ASHLEIGH BRILLIANT 2005.
ashleigh Brilliant.com
POT-SHOTS NO. 9946.
MACHINES MAKE US POWERFUL~
NOW ALL WE NEED IS A MACHINE TO MAKE US WISE.

©ASHLEIGH BRILLIANT 2005.
POT-SHOTS NO. 9881.
WHY CAN'T SOME CLEVER INVENTOR
COMBINE ALL THE WORLD'S DIFFERENT DEVICES
INTO ONE ALL-PURPOSE MACHINE?
ashleigh Brilliant.com

©ASHLEIGH BRILLIANT 2003.
POT-SHOTS NO. 9069.
THE BUTTON IS A WONDERFUL DEVICE ~
BUT IT WOULD BE NOTHING WITHOUT THE BUTTONHOLE.
ashleigh Brilliant .com

©ASHLEIGH BRILLIANT 2001
POT-SHOTS NO. 8881.
WHICH NUMBER
IS EXACTLY HALF-WAY BETWEEN ZERO AND INFINITY?
ashleigh Brilliant.com

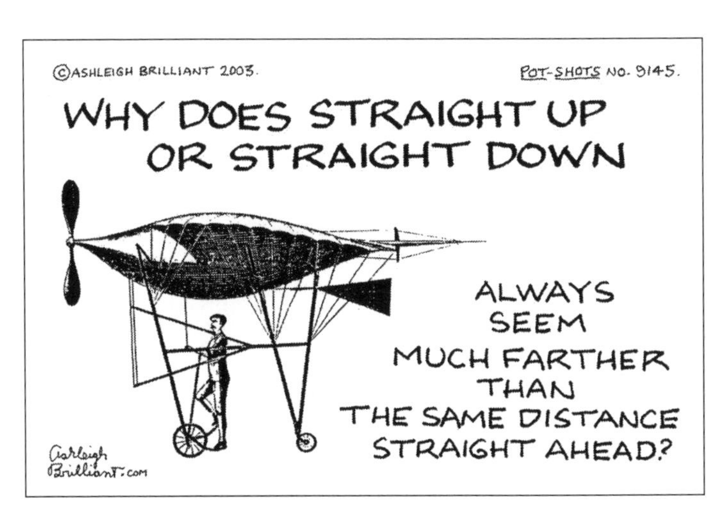
©ASHLEIGH BRILLIANT 2003.
POT-SHOTS NO. 9145.
WHY DOES STRAIGHT UP OR STRAIGHT DOWN
ALWAYS SEEM MUCH FARTHER THAN THE SAME DISTANCE STRAIGHT AHEAD?
ashleigh Brilliant.com

©ASHLEIGH BRILLIANT 2003.
POT-SHOTS NO. 9123.
INSECTS ARE EASY TO ADMIRE AND RESPECT,
BUT NOT SO EASY TO LOVE.
ashleigh Brilliant.com

©ASHLEIGH BRILLIANT 2003.
POT-SHOTS NO. 9640.
I TRUST SOME PEOPLE MORE THAN SOME MACHINES,
AND SOME MACHINES MORE THAN SOME PEOPLE.
ashleigh Brilliant.com

©ASHLEIGH BRILLIANT 2003.
POT-SHOTS NO. 9224.
ANTICIPATING
A
PLEASURE
CAN BE
THE
BEST PART.
ashleighbrilliant.com

©ASHLEIGH BRILLIANT 2001
POT-SHOTS NO. 8889.
WHAT DO WE WANT?
TOMORROW!
WHEN DO WE WANT IT?
NOW!
ashleigh
brilliant
.com

12. In Your Own Sweet Time

Congratulations! You have now (I optimistically presume) read your way through eleven chapters of sometimes very heavy thoughts. As your reward, we will lighten up in this final fandango, and focus our attention upon some of this multi-faceted world's brighter, sweeter facets. Perhaps — if I can determine its coordinates — I may even manage to locate and tickle your funny-bone.

Never let it be said — so I won't say it. What I will say is that many happy thoughts are floating around out there, waiting for somebody to think them.

And among the activities which seem to give meaning to life, pleasure-seeking is not to be scoffed at, even though some people's ideas of having a good time may seem to some others at best to be a waste of it, and at worst reminiscent of what has been reported about goings-on in the outer precincts of Hell.

But, as one great religious leader put it, "Let not your hearts be troubled." Surely, in this great cosmic casualty-ward, there is room — not to say need — for smiles and laughter, for fun and frivolity— even for downright silliness. After all, no convincing proof has yet been produced that life is not essentially intended to make fools of us all.

POT-SHOTS NO. 9395.

I THOUGHT
I TOLD YOU
TO HAVE
A GOOD
TIME!

AshleighBrilliant.com

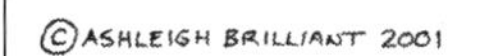

POT-SHOTS NO. 8813.

HOW AM I SOMETIMES ABLE TO DO THINGS BY CHANCE,

WHICH I COULD NEVER DO BY TRYING?

AshleighBrilliant.com

©ASHLEIGH BRILLIANT 1999. SANTA BARBARA.

POT-SHOTS NO. 8257.

UNSUCCESSFUL WRITER ALSO FAILS AT SUICIDE:

BULLET IS DEFLECTED BY WAD OF REJECTION LETTERS IN HIS POCKET.

www.AshleighBrilliant.com

©ASHLEIGH BRILLIANT 2003.

POT-SHOTS NO. 9459.

OUR TEAM IS STRUGGLING DESPERATELY

TO ESTABLISH A ONE-GAME WINNING STREAK.

AshleighBrilliant.com

 POT-SHOTS NO. 9313.

THINK HOW MUCH GREAT LITERATURE WOULD NEVER HAVE BEEN PRODUCED,

IF THE WRITERS HAD RECEIVED PROPER MEDICATION.

AshleighBrilliant.com

 POT-SHOTS NO. 9509.

AREN'T YOU GLAD THERE ARE SO MANY BOOKS

WHICH YOU WILL NEVER BE REQUIRED TO READ.

AshleighBrilliant.com

 POT-SHOTS NO. 8222.

ENJOYING LIFE

IS A GOOD IDEA ~

BUT IT SHOULDN'T BE THE ONLY IDEA IN YOUR HEAD.

www.AshleighBrilliant.com

©ASHLEIGH BRILLIANT 2003. POT-SHOTS NO. 9218.

THERE'S A BETTER TIME COMING ~

ITS NAME IS LUNCH.

ashleigh Brilliant.com

©ASHLEIGH BRILLIANT 2001
POT-SHOTS NO. 8844.
AshleighBrilliant.com
I WILL NEVER KILL,
SO LONG AS THERE IS ANY OTHER WAY TO GET CHOCOLATE.

©ASHLEIGH BRILLIANT 2003.
POT-SHOTS NO. 9539.
IT'S MY LUCKY DAY!
I'M ALIVE!
AshleighBrilliant.com

©ASHLEIGH BRILLIANT 1999 SANTA BARBARA.
POT-SHOTS NO. 8431.
HOW CAN SO MUCH SONG
COME OUT OF SUCH LITTLE BIRDS?
www.AshleighBrilliant.com

©ASHLEIGH BRILLIANT 1999. SANTA BARBARA. POT-SHOTS NO. 8479.

BOTHERING OLDER PEOPLE

IS HALF THE FUN OF BEING YOUNG.

www.AshleighBrilliant.com

©ASHLEIGH BRILLIANT 2003. POT-SHOTS NO. 9540.

GOOD CRITICS

ARE KNOWN TO BE GOOD

ONLY BECAUSE CRITICS TOO HAVE THEIR CRITICS.

AshleighBrilliant.com

©ASHLEIGH BRILLIANT 1999. SANTA BARBARA. POT-SHOTS NO. 8676.

A THOUSAND MILE JOURNEY BEGINS WITH ONE STEP ~

www.AshleighBrilliant.com

SO, TO SAVE 1000 MILES,

DON'T TAKE THAT STEP!

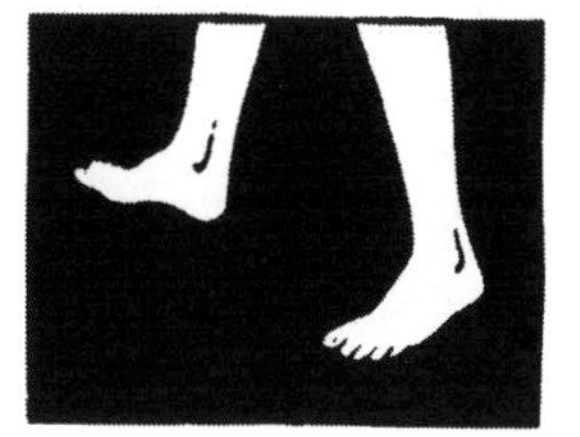

POT-SHOTS NO. 8794.

Why is the shortest way

not usually the same as the scenic route?

AshleighBrilliant.com

POT-SHOTS NO. 9720.

NO MATTER HOW SMALL A PART YOU PLAY,

IT MAY STILL BE AN ESSENTIAL ONE.

AshleighBrilliant.com

POT-SHOTS NO. 8929.

IT'S POSSIBLE TO HAVE MANY DESTINATIONS ~

BUT YOU CAN ONLY REACH ONE AT A TIME.

AshleighBrilliant.com

©ASHLEIGH BRILLIANT 2003.
POT-SHOTS NO. 9056.
IF THIS IS ALL ACTUALLY HAPPENING,
THEN I MUST REALLY BE ALIVE!
AshleighBrilliant.com

©ASHLEIGH BRILLIANT 2005.
POT-SHOTS NO.9772.
WHY DO PEOPLE WITH LESS
SO OFTEN SEEM HAPPIER THAN PEOPLE WITH MORE?
AshleighBrilliant.com

©ASHLEIGH BRILLIANT 2005
POT-SHOTS NO. 9978.
THE PROBLEM IS:
HOW TO SATISFY YOUR AUDIENCE,
BUT STILL LEAVE THEM WANTING MORE.
AshleighBrilliant.com

Part Time:

Yes, it's time for us to part. But this separation need only be part-time. In these days of instantaneous communication and a multitude of media, my Brilliant Thoughts can circulate in ways that words and images were never before capable of. So, I hope that, here and there, we'll keep meeting each other, perhaps in unexpected places. As an example of what can happen, not long ago I heard from a soldier at a U.S. military base, whose job there was to process the belongings of service men and women who had been killed overseas. Among one person's effects, he found one of my books. Until then, he'd never heard of me, and had been totally unaware of my work, but was now so enthralled by it that he felt he had to write and tell me of how he made this discovery.

Whatever the circumstances, whether it happens in print or online, on an office wall or somebody's refrigerator, in a library or bookstore, or among the forgotten items in an old attic, here's hoping we'll meet again...and again.

In the meantime, we must endure the sweet sorrow of parting. You are off to do whatever people do when they put this book aside. I, for my part, remain comfortably here in these pages, patiently waiting.

Many languages have very similar parting expressions —"Au Revoir," "Auf Wiedersehen," and "Hasta la Vista,"— all look forward to the next meeting. And even our "Goodbye," though it sounds more final, is just an abbreviated way of saying "God be with you, until we meet again."

So, the thought is really always the same. And let it be the same for you and me: Here's to the next time!

Pot-Shots
BY ASHLEIGH BRILLIANT
I HATE TO SAY
GOODBYE
SO I WON'T
POT-SHOTS NO. 112
© BRILLIANT ENTERPRISES 1969
Ashleigh Brilliant

About the Author:

ASHLEIGH BRILLIANT
Epigrammatist

"During my 30s, in the 1960s, it occurred to me that very short writing was a literary area worth exploring. I have been most influenced by two anonymous schools of writing: (1) the creators of commercial advertising and (2)the people who write on walls."

Ashleigh Brilliant 2007

Brilliant grew up in London and graduated from the University of London with honors. He then attended college in California, earning his teaching credential and MA in Education from Claremont College and his PhD in History from UC Berkeley. He taught history at Chapman's "Floating University" for two years and at a community college in Oregon

In addition to being a syndicated cartoonist, Ashleigh Brilliant has served as a newspaper columnist, as an illustrator for two books, and as an author of several books on subjects ranging from the Southern California's car craze of the 1920s, to personal essays, to a Haight-Ashbury Songbook. He even recorded a live album in Golden Gate Park in 1967, *Ashleigh Brilliant in the Haight-Ashbury*.

This is his tenth book of Brilliant Thoughts — a collection of his universally beloved "Pot-Shots."

Among his many awards and encomiums, Brilliant has been the recipient of the Distinguished Alumnus Award from Claremont Graduate University in 1987, and the Raymond B. Bragg Award for Humanism in Entertainment and the Arts.

If that wasn't enough, in December 2013 on his 80th birthday, the mayor of his hometown Santa Barbara, presented him with a signed document officially proclaiming Ashleigh Brilliant to be the "Wise Old Man of the Mountain."

Manufactured by Amazon.ca
Bolton, ON

10277251R00092